Albert Rowe Barlow

Company G. : a record of the services of one company of the 157th N. Y. vols. in the war of the rebellion, from Sept. 19, 1862 to July 10, 1865

Including the roster of the company

Albert Rowe Barlow

Company G. : a record of the services of one company of the 157th N. Y. vols. in the war of the rebellion, from Sept. 19, 1862 to July 10, 1865
Including the roster of the company

ISBN/EAN: 9783337207779

Printed in Europe, USA, Canada, Australia, Japan

Cover: Foto ©ninafisch / pixelio.de

More available books at **www.hansebooks.com**

A RECORD OF THE SERVICES OF ONE COMPANY OF THE 157TH N. Y. VOLS. IN THE WAR OF THE REBELLION.

FROM SEPT. 19, 1862, TO JULY 10, 1865.

INCLUDING THE ROSTER OF THE COMPANY.

BY A. R. BARLOW.

A. W. HALL, Publisher,
Syracuse, N. Y.
1899.

PREFATORY.

The production of this little work has long been contemplated. It has seemed right that the records of some of the volunteer organizations sent from Canastota and vicinity, during the War of the Rebellion, should be recorded in such a form as would preserve to the families of those boys, their deeds in marching, in fighting, in suffering for the old flag. In an effort to accomplish such an undertaking as this, the patronage of the general public is not considered. The book, if requiting for the expense of publication, will be considered a success financially.

As a literary effort, no claim is filed, unless one is admissable for general accuracy in the matter of events and dates. Some critics may take exception to the attempt herein made, to individualize a collective noun and yet retain plurality; and in the same measure, pervert mood and tense. It is admitted that the license is unique. Quite likely other departures from good old grammatical paths will be noted. Let it be remembered, however, that the experiences of Co. G were, as a whole, unique, and to harmonize the literal with the actual, the record should be drawn uniquely.

No apology is offered for trivial treatment of some of the subjects; in truth, they are deserving of severe handling. If lack of respect for commanding officers is shown, the explanation given is, that they have been removed from the high pedestals of war-gods and are considered only as men.

It is in no bitter sense the men who fought Co. G are termed rebels. They were in rebellion and were known to the boys as rebels, or johnny rebs. A false delicacy only would prompt the writer to deprive those Southern men of a title which, apparently, they bore with pride.

As stated, this is not a work for the public eye. It is an offering to comrades, from a comrade who marched with them, and experienced with them the fortunes and misfortunes of war. And in performing this work, care has been taken to omit such occurrences as might not be understood by others than the actors; and while thus

PREFATORY.

avoiding over-coloring by a faithful portraiture of events, and suppressing nothing worthy of record Co. G go into history.

In performing this duty, individual names have been used, illustrative of passing events. Should any person feel aggrieved over such freedom, let it be known, it was, indeed, born of familiarity with the subjects, and is indulged in a spirit of good comradeship, without thought of disparagement.

No man who marched with those boys can think of them unkindly. If there were ever differences of a serious nature, the writer is unmindful of them.

To travel over the old roads, to hunger and to thirst again; to sleep where night found them; in sunshine, in storm out on the picket-line; to toss upon a bed of suffering and weaken, day by day, for lack of tender care;—in brief, to march away to the wars and enjoy the rich compensation of an honorable return, all this and more, has been lived again while preparing this record. And so with the old boys, as long as they live, will they by this effort be enabled to travel Virginia roads in all kinds of weather, without danger of sticking fast in the mud, or of being stifled amid clouds of gray dust.

Why Co. G did not cut a broader swath along the pathway of glorious attainment, they cannot understand. They were a willing body of men, and were of a regiment of noble hearts. Misfortunes of war, simply, were not the only elements at work defeating their best endeavors. The true causes can be learned, only, in a huge compendium of tragical, whimsical and amusing facts, concealed within the folios of that unwritten or mythical history of the war, which never will be published, a history that would tumble war-idols to the ground, and elevate men who have passed into obscurity.

But Co. G have never permitted their escutcheon to lie prone in the dust, that they might more readily engage in wrangling over such small matters as position and preference. They do not grumble, they do not boast. They learned, thirty-five years ago, to accept the inevitable, which has been awarded to them in large quantities.

Co. G were boys of Lenox, who served in the name of Lenox. They belonged, then to Lenox, as her offering in the war, and their record is a part of the history of the town. Divested of verbiage, their deeds will still be found honorable and manly. For, as once said the lamented Capt. Frank, Co. G did "as well as any of them."

A few words should be given in memory of the dead, who, in life, stood shoulder to shoulder with the boys of Co. G. Dead?—a word applied to express a religious belief; but how inexpressive of a new-birth.

"Death is but another name for change.
The weary shuffle off their mortal coil,
And think to slumber in eternal night.
But, lo! the man, tho' dead is living still;
Unclothed, is clothed upon, and his Mortality
Is swallowed up of Life."

Thus sang an inspired woman, and thus shall it be said of the boys who gave their lives for the flag, and for their comrades who shall follow them. And some day, upon the great plain of Light, the hosts will once more marshal for a grand review.

ROSTER OF CO. G, 157TH N. Y. VOLS.

CAPTAINS.
Abraham Tuttle.
*Harrison Frank.
**Lafayette McWilliams.

LIEUTENANTS.
Maurice D. Bailey.
Harrison Frank.
Marshall Hemstreet.
**Frank E. Gates.
**Robert E. Grant.
**Jerome Forbes.
Clark Pierce.

ORDERLY SERGEANTS.
Israel P. Moore.
Marshall Hemstreet,
Frank E. Gates.
**John H. Roe.
Jerome Forbes.
Hubbard Suits.

SERGEANTS.

    Marshall Hemstreet.
    Frank E. Gates.
    Henry C. Jarvis.
    John H. Roe.
    James B. Hooper.
**Nicholas Binges.
    John H. Fancher.
    Wm. H. Barlow.
**Harvey Lindsley.

CORPORALS.

    Jerome Forbes.
**Irwin A. Sayles.
**James B. Hooper.
    Clarence L. Spencer.
**Asa E. New.
    Wm. J. Peck.
    Wm. H. Barlow.
    Nicholas Binges.
    Hubbard Suits.
**Charles A. Near.
 . Daniel A. Betsinger
**Albert R. Barlow.
**Jerry Murphy.
**William Miller.
    Wm. H. Kimball.

MUSICIAN.
W. H. Perry.
TEAMSTER.
Wm. G. Johnson.
COOKS.
William Mallows.
Ziba Cloyes.
Patrick Matthews.
PRIVATES.
**Amos Avery.
**Peter Agan.
Daniel A. Betsinger.
Wm. W. Baldwin.
*Albert D. Bridge.
Daniel Brockway
Albert R. Barlow.
Ziba Cloyes.
Alfred J. Cole.
Peter Cummings.
Francis H. Carey.
John H. Dunham.
Nicholas Ecker.
*John W. Foltz.
Conrad Foltz.
**Robert Farrington.
John H. Fancher.
Francis M. Gault.

Daniel D. Grovestien.
Stephen D. Harrington.
Joseph H. Hart.
*John A. Hart.
Jacob Hallicus.
***James M. Hainsworth.
**James Johnson.
*Luzerne E. Johnson.
Henry Kellogg.
Harvey Lindsley.
*Asa C. Lawrence.
Luther Loucks.
Wm. Mallows.
Myron A. Menzie.
Henry Mason.
Patrick Matthews.
James Matthews.
Jerry Murphy.
*Durell Moore.
Jeremiah McLane.
**John J. McMaster.
**William Miller.
**John Miller.
**Michael Miller.
**Chas. A. Near.
**Simon Nestler.
**Hugh O'Brien.

*Francis C. Pratt.
**William Pease.
**John Pfleiger.
Mason Phelps.
Chas. O. Ricker.
Wm. E. Rinn.
***Henry W. Richardson.
Nicholas J. Snyder.
Eusebius Sweet
Hubbard Suits.
**James L. Travis.
John Torrey.
Elmer A. Wise.
*Alfred Wilder.
**Henry Whaling.
Calvin White.

DRAFTED RECRUITS.
Geo. S. Orr.
Scott D. Whitney.

SUBSTITUTES FOR DRAFTED MEN.
James Leonard.
John Wise.

ENLISTED AS RECRUITS.
*Abram Thornton.
Sylvanus D. Alexander.
Peter Delong.
Chas. Hoxie.

Nelson Kimball.
Henry Nobles.
Sylvanus S. Ostrander.
Samuel N. Jacquay.
*Russell Stroup.
Paul Stowell.
Wm. H. Schuyler.
Levi Schuyler.
Chas. O. Hinman.
**Wm. L. Johnson.
Wm. H. Kimball.
Patrick Kinney.
Alfred J. Leird.
William Rudd.
John Terry.
Daniel Winchell.
John Brown.
George Plank.
Arthur Campbell.
Rufus C. Baldwin.

---

*Killed in Action.
**Wounded.
***Died by disease or accident.

COMPANY G.

The date of their captain's commission placed Co. G seventh in rank—beginning with A—and ninth company from the extreme right as the regiment formed on the colors. The company was enrolled and became a part of the 157th regiment of New York Volunteers, enlisted for three years unless sooner discharged—"for three years unless sooner shot," according to Irwin Sayles, who left the company and the service minus a right arm. The regiment was raised in Cortland and Madison Counties, under the call of July 2d, 1862, for 300,000 three years men.

ABRAHAM TUTTLE, the first captain of Co. G, was a farmer living near Clockville. He was about forty years of age, slightly gray, but strong and active. Capt. Tuttle was an old-time California gold-seeker, who took the long route via, Cape Horn to the then new Eldorado. In some respects he was well fitted for a soldier, but he had no taste for such a life, as a profession, and resigned after experiencing the discomforts of a winter campaign in Virginia.

MAURICE D. BAILEY, of Wampsville, was first lieutenant of Co. G. He was one of the handsomest men in the regiment—finely made and set-up in good style and in the prime and vigor of life. He was a big-hearted man and popular. At home he was a farmer. After serving with the company for a few months, he was assigned to Co. K, being promoted to a captaincy, and remained with the regiment until the autumn of 1863, when he resigned, at Folly Island, S. C.

HARRISON FRANK, second lieutenant of Co. G, was a speculator in farm produce and lived at Wampsville; he was thirty-two years of age, a rather tall, spare-built man. He came from German stock, and his grandfather, Albert Frank, was a soldier of the Revolution. His maternal grandfather, George Siver, was a soldier of 1812. Andrew Frank married Nancy Siver and Harrison Frank was their son.

So it appears that Harrison was born with a martial spirit in him. Unfortunately his physical powers were too frail for the hardships of camp and field. It would seem that only a strong will power supported the man for weeks at a time. "I will never give up until I am down," was written on every line of his features, while his figure was unsteady and his limbs seemed unfit for carrying his body. But his eye was clear and his voice rang out sharp and authoritative. He possessed a shrill tone of voice, was rapid in speech, his perceptions were clear, his preferences leaning to that which was just and right; was methodical, correct, generous, temperate. Cared little for the glitter of military display and wore on parade the dress coat of a private adorned with shoulder straps. This was not from penuriousness. One day the colonel took him to task for not appearing in a uniform coat.

"Colonel," he replied, "I have a mother and others at home, who need all I can save from my pay. In my baggage I have a new uniform coat. My boys know me in this uniform."

He wore that plain dress coat unmolested. In fact, when he fell at Gettysburg he wore the ordinary blouse of a private soldier, with two bars attached, taken from an old shoulder strap.

When Frank was made captain, the discipline of Co. G was very indifferent, their tactics none of the best. They needed inspiring and the right sort of man took hold of them, who knew there was crude material in his company, of such from which good soldiers were produced; so he applied himself and with immediate results, to make Co. G one of the good companies of the regiment. Frank had been left behind when the regiment went to the front. He was in poor health, but finally reached Washington and lay there in hospital, or under treatment, for weeks, rejoining the boys at Fairfax Court House, Va. He was still weak, but brimful of patriotism, was sanguine of victory for the North and said he expected to march into Richmond. Such sort of grit served him to the last. Gradually, as the winter gave place to balmy spring, his health seemed to improve and with that encouraging condition came his ability to convey to his men the ambition of the soldier; and it was not long before Co. G were looking up handsomely. In April, 1863, President Lincoln reviewed the Army of the Potomac then lying in the vicinity of Falmouth. Co. G were bright under the applications of tripoli polish, blacking and brush-brooming; new uniforms, white gloves, etc.

Capt. Frank was proud of his men. As their esprit improved the men grew to liking more and more the man who sought their greatest good.

In this connection it is only just to remember a patriotic act of Mrs. Daniel Crouse, of Canastota, who presented a regulation sword to each of the officers of Co. G. The ceremony occurred in the old Dutch Reformed Church in Canastota. Judge Barlow made the presentation speech, to which the then Lieutenant Frank responded in a modest, but manly style.

A FEW NOTES OF GENERAL INTEREST.

Co. G was recruited in the middle portion of the Town of Lenox, Madison County. It was known in the regiment as the Canastota Company. A patriotic region was the territory within a radius of four miles of that small village. Before 1856 it was counted a reliably Democratic locality, but the anti-slavery agitation soon found it fertile ground for propagating Free-Soil ideas and it rapidly changed to the Republican side, as soon as the issue was fairly made. So, when the war broke out, the missionary work of such men as Gerrit Smith, Samuel J. May, Beriah Green, and others, became apparent, and patriotism burned bright upon its rural altars. It is estimated that at least five hundred men were recruited within the territory already designated. The Town of Lenox paid

$136,030 for town bounties, while Madison County paid a total of $1,338,320 for bounties to recruits. Lenox paid for support of families $3,786, distinct from Poor Fund; both for bounties and for relief thus raised by tax, Lenox shows double that of any other town in the county. And those figures do not by any means represent the thousands of dollars voted at the recruiting meetings and subscribed and donated for local bounties and for relief purposes.

Very pleasant to recall are the kind words spoken and written in those trying times by noble-hearted men and women, as the boys went forth to the war.

In August, 1862, a war fund was raised in Madison County. Hon. Gerrit Smith, with his usual generosity, promptly sent in his check for $5,000, and in his note which enclosed the same, he says—"I would that the fund should not be regarded as a mercenary appeal to our volunteers—but as a gift from loving neighbors toward helping them to arrange their affairs that they can leave their homes more freely and pleasantly. These volunteers and their neighbors constitute a partnership sacred and sublime, and never to be broken."

Canastota was very active and like many other

towns at the time, doing unceasingly for the men in the field, for local relief and in support of the good cause generally. It is doubtful if any locality in the State, with the same population and a like assessment, can show a more honorable record.

It should be noted that at least fifty per cent. of the men enlisted in 1862 were at the time beardless youths, the greater portion of whom proved enduring soldiers. Those boys did not enlist for sake of obtaining bounties. Enthusiasm was aroused in various ways—by speeches at war-meetings, by martial music and by the newspapers. Everybody talked war, the girls sang war songs, one boy enlisted and his chums followed him. Very little cared those young fellows for bounties. The county of Madison gave $50, and the State $50, bounties. One month's pay in advance $13, and $2 bonus from the general government and $100 at the expiration of the term of service (increased after the war to $200). In the fall of 1864 the town of Lenox gave for bounties to 3-years men $1,100, the county $500 added to that, besides the State and national bounties, and many of those men never were in a battle.

But the trials of war were not entirely with

the boys at the front. Dependent parents, wives and children felt the denials keenly; and when news came that a battle had been fought and some of their boys had fallen, the entire community was interested at once and freely sympathized with sorrowing friends. And the firm belief that they were thus cared for strengthened the boys wonderfully.

Of the eighty-seven men originally enrolled in Co. G, one-half of them were between the ages of eighteen and twenty-one years, and no doubt a number of them several years below the minimum age of eighteen, fearing rejection, assumed to be older.

The fatalities of war among those volunteers are difficult to estimate. Not a few were reported as "missing," who never returned. Many of the sick and wounded lived to see their homes and soon after died.

During its term of service the company lost one captain and six enlisted men killed in action, and one man accidently shot, while three died of disease. The man Asa Lawrence, missing at Chancellorsville, is included among the killed, and according to all that has been learned, he has never been heard from. One captain, three lieutenants and twenty-four men, were wounded. Of the original enrollment sixteen were discharged on account of sickness or wounds, five were discharged to accept commissions and five were transferred to the Invalid corps. Nine men deserted. Forty-two enlisted men returned with the regiment, others not present were still borne on the rolls.

The company during its term received accessions of two substitutes, two drafted men and twenty-four recruits. Of those, several were slightly wounded and two died of disease.

The casualties in Co. G were not as many as in some of the companies of the regiment. Co. C lost seven killed and more than forty wounded. Co. I lost one officer and eight men killed and their captain and twenty-nine men wounded.

It was understood at the time the authorization was issued that the company was to be assigned to a regiment forming of Cortland and Madison County men, with Philip P. Brown, Jr., of Hamilton, as colonel, and to rendezvous at Hamilton. As rapidly as possible the enlistments were pushed along and about two weeks from the time recruiting began, the company was assured of its quota and took its name as Company G.

At Hamilton, the camp was established on the fair grounds north of the village. For a time a large tent afforded shelter to the men, but its capacity being insufficient, five barrack buildings were erected on the west side of the enclosure, two companies in each building. Co. G shared in the shelter of the most northerly barrack and in the west section of the building, with Co. B, their neighbors, in the eastern portion. Two tiers of bunks ranged along each side of the structure and each bunk was occupied by two men; at the entrance was a room for commissioned officers, most of whom preferred the softer beds in the hotels of the village to the hard straw ticks of the camp.

As the recruits arrived in town they were taken to one of the public halls, where surgeons Hendrick, Beebe and Crawe hammered their chests, listened to their heartbeats and respiration, looked into the eyes of the recruits, finally ordering them to jump over the floor on each leg consecutively. During this ordeal the boys appeared in the uniform of Nature only. Few failed to pass the Board, however, and the successful ones then appeared before the adjutant. If a minor, a written consent was required from the parent or guardian.

Accepted recruits were given orders upon the quartermaster and were taken over to a warehouse near the canal and there received an outfit. The dress coat of dark blue, also dark blue flannel blouse and pants, overcoat, coarse gray shirts, canton flannel drawers, woolen socks, shoes and blanket, not to forget the dark blue fatigue cap so heartily disliked by the wearers. The civilian garb was shed at once and the green soldier was revealed in the cut and fit of his new clothing of war, while his back itched under those shirts as though numerous flies and ants were perambulating there, with an occasioned nipping from a stray spider. But how very, very verdant the boys appeared—so harmless-like in their uniforms, and to add to the ludicrous feature of the occasion very many of them hastened to a gallery to have their appearance preserved for all time.

Knapsacks, haversacks and canteens, tin cups and plates, knives and spoons, came to each in time. No guns were issued in Camp Mitchell; guards about the camp carried guns borrowed from a local armory—no cartridges were issued. A high board fence presented the most discouraging barricade to such of the boys as desired a night outside.

It was amusing to observe the schemes for gaining liberty and to see the boys return to duty after a day or two in the narrow quarters of the guard house. They were not accustomed to such discipline; but they were soon to learn that they had entered upon a new career.

Life in barracks was not tedious. During the day there were several marching drills by squad, platoon and company, and in the evening dress parade, and perhaps, a few attempts at battalion evolutions. Officers in nearly every company were as green as the men. A few short-enlistment men who had seen service and returned, and some who had served in home companies, usually were the drill-masters. Col. Brown had been captain of the Hamilton Grays; Major Carmichael for a time served as captain in the 76th N. Y.; a few other officers had been in the service.

Co. G were drilled by Sergeants Hemstreet and Gates, six months' recruits to the 12th N. Y. V.; also by Frank Cooper afterwards a member of the 78th N. Y. During drill hours "hay-foot, straw-foot!"—"heels together, toes on a line, body erect resting on the toes,"—"forward, march!" and "halt,"—the orders from drill-masters, were heard on all sides; and over in one corner of the pen were the ten or more fifers and drummers taking first lessons in martial music. The scene was enough to make an old soldier weep from laughter, and yet it was not an unusual one wherever raw troops were mustered.

The eating house at Camp Mitchell (so named in honor of David J. Mitchell, a lawyer, at one time a resident of Hamilton) stood at the east end of the enclosure, into which the men were marched by their officers, three times daily to their meals. Good, wholesome fare was provided and in abundance and would have been pronounced grand one year later, could those boys have obtained it on Folly Island, in place of wormy hardtack and tough salt-horse.

The sick at Hamilton were quartered in a small church near the grounds, but Co. G were fortunate as to health while at the rendezvous. Many of the boys enjoyed furloughs during those five or six weeks and their friends visited them and were often permitted to pass the night at the barracks. Amusements of various kinds broke the monotony of barrack life—card playing, wrestling, quoits, various games and much rough horse-play, continually in sight.

While there was so much life astir in Camp Mitchell, it must be acknowledged that a few of the men were down-hearted, particularly those about to leave wives and children; and who could blame them? There were heavy hearts in the homes of those boys. One man when called upon to give a written consent for his sons to enlist, remarked that he felt as if he were signing their death-warrants. For there was a terrible uncertainty for soldiers in those days and the much-quoted silver lining of the heavy clouds overhanging our country, was yet to be discovered in the future efforts of her loyal sons. Cripples and sick men were returning from the front and occasionally somebody's child was brought home for burial. The failure of the Peninsula Campaign, followed by the disaster at Bull Run, were bad records, scarcely effaced by the hard-earned victory at Antietam. And yet, amid such desolation the American people of the North never ceased to give of blood and treasure and the boys kept marching on, the matrons and the maidens smiling and waving farewells with hearts and eyes overflowing, the men and boys cheering, bands playing, fifes shrieking and drums beating. The boys marched away, the hospitals filled, little mounds dotted many a Southern field, the ranks thinned and the scene was repeated again and again until victory came; and then it was time to count the cost. Those who suffered were the ones to cast the reckoning.

On the 19th of September, 1862, the regiment was mustered into the service of the United States. The preliminary of scanning-over the men was performed during a dreary rain storm, by regular army surgeons, the men in line by company. Few were rejected and those for defects of eyes or teeth, or for manifest feebleness. There was Ziba Cloyes of Co. G, a man of sixty years, who had enlisted as being only forty-four, gray hair and a general suspicion of advanced years about him. The surgeon reached him in the line.

"What is your age, sir?"

"Forty-four."

The surgeon smiled. "Open your mouth."

Ziba obeyed, disclosing a full set of teeth such as would have delighted many a dude. Then he brought them together with a sharp snap.

"Put your finger in there," he said, again opening his jaws to their widest limit.

"You will do, sir," said the surgeon as he passed, with a broad grin, to the next man.

After the examination came the formal muster-in by companies, and Co. G were then an arm of the government and on the direct road to active service. Orders thereafter emanated from officers of the general government and the State was duly accredited. Co. G. had saved Canastota from a draft.

Sept. 25th, with their new rubber-cloth knapsacks, haversacks and canteens, at an early hour, Co. G were mustered for the road. Teams had been generously offered by the people far and near, gratuitously, and on that morning to the number of more than one hundred blocked the streets of the village, long before daybreak, in waiting to carry the regiment to Canastota.

The loading was quite slow and consumed considerable time, but the day was fine and the roads in excellent condition and the journey to Peterboro was made without further delay. In that pleasant little village the regiment left the wagons and marched into the park, where tables were spread on the green and laden with good fare. While the boys were eating, they were favored with a speech from Hon. Gerrit Smith. He was seated upon a white horse. His deep, eloquent tones were heard above the clatter of dishes. It was his wish that the boys be not withheld from eating. Above his head waved the stars and stripes at half-mast, in memory of Capt. Barnett, killed at Antietam—a Peterboro boy. All that was saddening, all that was eloquent and nobly good in the place, was not so appealing just then, as the feast before them; the boys of Co. G were hungry. After the feast and the address of welcome and God-speed, the wagons were again mounted.

The long train reached Canastota about 5 p. m. They were unloaded south of the town and the men given their first experience with those handsome new knapsacks, as they marched (bent forward like pack-peddlers) through the village streets. It was their first experience, also, in straggling—the head of the regiment led by the Hamilton band, was approaching the Peterboro St. bridge as the rear of the column passed into Center St., strung nearly around the square.

A platform had been built in a field north of the Crouse residence and near the railroad. Prominent citizens of Cortland and Madison were on the platform; Gen. Bruce was speaker. Guards were thrown around the enclosure to keep the crowd outside, but not to exclude the relatives and friends. Caresses and sobbing, tears and forced gaity marked that occasion.

Little ones were there and the father fed himself with one hand as he pressed his child to his breast with the other. Old age came also, and parents trembling with years, tried to be brave as their part in the war, if nothing more. Even the abundance of choice food supplied for the men was hardly relished under the strain of parting; so the women filled the haversacks, poured coffee into the canteens, completing the whole with a hearty kiss and sent the boys on their way. There were times, when the happiest soldier boy was he, who, when going to war, left none at home to weep for him.

A train of emigrant cars received the regiment and at daybreak next morning they reached Albany. A good breakfast was served in a building near the depot. A portion of the regiment was taken over the ferry and the remainder, including Co. G, marched to the executive mansion where Gov. Morgan presented the stand of colors, D. J. Mitchell responding.

The boys will ever remember their ride down the rail along the Hudson. At every station and in homes along the road, in the fields and on the river, wherever men, women or children were seen, their handkerchiefs and hats were waved to cheer the soldier boys. The boys in blue threw kisses to the blushing girls, or upon brown paper or pieces cut from lunch boxes, wrote and cast forth gentle words of appreciation. Really it must have grown monotonous to those people, as soldiers were passing nearly every day; if so, it was such a monotony as they appeared to enjoy immensely. With some of the men of Co. G the situation was too serious for trifling—they were leaving their Marias and Nancys and Kates.

City Hall barracks, New York City—never forget them. The postoffice building now covers that ground. Bunks floored with slats to sleep upon, into which the many occupants had crawled, each time carrying in from the floors a fresh supply of sand to fall into the eyes of the fellows in the lower berths; the rooms ill-ventilated and odorous of many stalwart smells. The food was unattractive and few of Co. G had the hardihood to partake. Just one cheering feature of the situation, was the hope ever constant, that their stay would be brief. They stopped but one night and a day. As evening approached they were marched down to a covered dock and remained there in the dark, unlighted place, awaiting the arrival of a steamer to take them over to Jersey.

Soon as darkness came on the men became very quiet as though the bogie-man was abroad. By and by a clicking, cracking sort of noise came out of the depths of darkness, soon followed by a smacking sound. Co. G were eating cheese—the other companies were eating cheese.

"Commandants of companies will see that their men are kept together," roared the colonel.

The officers could not see very well in the dark. The men broke open no more cheese boxes. They had spied the boxes through the gathering gloom on their first arrival and simply waited patiently for darkness.

John Shultz, a German, and member of Co. G, had sat himself down on the outer timber of the wharf and fell asleep. He had not removed his knapsack. What his canteen contained is not known. He nodded awhile, snored a little and suddenly disappeared. Some one raised the cry that a man had fallen into the slip. A police boat picked old John out and soon he returned, thoroughly wet and considerably sobered.

Near midnight a steamer reached the wharf and took the regiments away to Port Monmouth, the northern terminus of the Delaware and Raritan Bay R. R. Once more the raiding propensities of the boys were exhibited upon a carload of peaches on a siding, but they were promptly restrained. The men were not thieves; they had somehow reached the conclusion that a change in dress demanded a change in morals. They knew there was some sort of transformation going on within them, as without, and certainly they must act differently than when they were plain civilians. Instead of being peaceful lambs at home, they must be wolves and hunt in packs. But a few months of strict discipline set them aright.

It was Sunday afternoon when the regiment reached Philadelphia, tired and hungry. A lunch had been served on the train early in the day, but that was only a "hand-out." At Philadelphia many thousands of men of passing regiments, were fed at the Cooper's Union refreshment rooms. So Co. G, though only one-tenth of a regiment, were favored with plenty of clean water, soap and towels and then were served with a delicious meal of good substantial food, served on a clean cloth, from earthen dishes, "just like home," said the boys.

Philadelphia always treated the soldiers in the

most generous style. A sick or wounded man felt greatly favored to be sent to a Philadelphia hospital.

After the regiment was fed, the march was taken for the Baltimore depot, several miles distant. The walks were crowded with people. Such cheering, waving handkerchiefs, tossing of kisses, helped mightily in the struggle beneath those galling knapsacks. Some of the giddy girls rushed up to the ranks and exchanged handkerchiefs bearing their names; others tossed flowers among the boys, and "good-by," "God bless you," was heard, from the start to the finish.

The cars in waiting were ordinary cattle cars, in which rough board seats were built. This was the first acquaintance the men had with such sort of conveyance. For the officers, a coach was provided, but many of them remained with their men.

In the recent war with Spain, coaches were provided for the men; and for the sick, sleeping cars and dining cars, all of which was perfectly right. Between Washington and any portion of the eastern and Middle states, no soldier, during the War of the Rebellion, should have been obliged to ride in a car built for cattle, particularly after the war had progressed for over one year.

At Baltimore the namby-pamby feature of the excursion ceased, Enfield rifles were dealt out to the companies, together with accoutrements, the cartridge box, belts, etc. That seemed like war. No cartridges were issued; those came on Arlington Hights.

The city of Baltimore had shown, to some extent, an inclination in favor of secession. Many of its young men had gone to the Confederate lines and a strong feeling against federal interference with secession was very noticeable among a certain class of the citizens. Troops were stationed there to preserve order.

The regiment was marched into an open street with guards stationed to prevent the men from wandering about the city. Co. G remained strictly passive within bounds and found no opportunity for doing otherwise. They were exemplary fellows when under guard.

An unusual place for a dining hall was that at Baltimore—on an upper floor near the depot. Very good food was supplied, particularly the coffee.

Co. G were very fond of coffee; although at that early day it had not become so necessary to those heroes in embryo as it was a few years later. The experience of soldiers generally in that war, favored the use of coffee. It was food as well as drink. When a fellow was nearly fagged, on a severe march, the mention of coffee appeared to brace him, and a hand would slip into the haversack for a pinch, only to tide him along. A spoonful of coffee in a canteen of water lifted one comfortably over many a weary mile. To abolish the whisky ration was wise. To have taken away the coffee would have endangered the cause.

Coffee and the letters from home were two important auxiliary supports of the nation. Those letters were a power. Nothing went just right when the mail was delayed. Anticipation is a great word and the soldiers worked it for all it is worth; on all the various grades of the psychic thermometer from zero to fever heat. Ah, when fever heat was struck, the indication was reliably certain that she had "gone back on" her soldier lad.

Clean cattle cars were supplied at Philadelphia, but the sort in which Co. G traveled from Baltimore to Washington were fragrant of stable odors. The distance was little over forty miles, yet the entire night was consumed. That scheme of traveling nights and loafing around half dead during the daytime, was never explained. Some of the men had a suspicion that Col. Brown was fearful that he might lose some of his men if he changed cars in the night time, and so corralled them the same as other stock. However that might have been, in his regiment the most remarkable desertions were among the officers.

Co. G did not enlist to become deserters and the few of them who did desert were scarcely missed; and a halo of glory which hung over the heroic Co. G at the close of the war obscured, if it did not eliminate, all weak points. Orators and newspapers accorded them glory, the popular cry glorified them. Why not place the laurel crown right here?

September 30th was a beautiful day, but warm in Washington. Co. G jumped down from their cattle cars and were marched to cattle barracks near the capitol. There was plenty of space for camping, but no tents had been issued to them. Those barracks terraced up the hill, resembled barns, rough boarded and whitewashed. The lawmakers over in the huge marble building nearby, reclined upon soft cushions. The sons of their constituents, who had come down to settle a serious difference stirred up in that building, were marched into foul-smelling barracks because they were soldiers. It was too bad to treat American troops that way.

At those barracks the feeding place for soldiers at that time was abominable in filth and mussiness. Coffee was served in what the boys named swill-pails, with a coating of grease outside and inside. The cooks and waiters bore hands and faces that lacked for soap and water. Many a bold soldier boy, after a peep into the feeding room, retired to a convenient refreshment saloon and bought his meals. As for Co. G, they said little but thought much, resolving that a revelation should appear as the years moved along, and even thus it is recorded, long after those slip-shod cooks have ceased to slop, and longer since the boys have any use for them. And now the vindictiveness of Co. G is spent.

Unfortunately, before Co. G could be taken out of Washington some of its members had filled themselves with poor liquor. The same fellows had given trouble while en route from the North, and on various occasions suspicious looking bottles were taken rfom them by the officers and thrown from the train. More shame for Co. G, who were not fighting under the banner of King Alcohol.

In the middle of the day column was formed and the boys marched out on Pennsylvania Avenue. Numbers of small boys flanked the line bargaining for the task of carrying knapsacks —carts were there for the same purpose and a brisk bargaining ensued. It was indeed a comfortable way to carry a knapsack—transferred to a cart or to the back of a negro boy. Thus disburdened, marching was easier. The air was hot, the roads very dusty. Across Long Bridge they went, past Forts Runion and Albany, to an old camp known as Camp Chase, nearly one mile in rear of the Lee mansion, on Arlington Hights. Old A tents were there, pitched and ready for occupation, true, not as clean as desirable, but a shelter which a little labor of dusting and arranging greatly improved.

Routine is the term expressive of life in camp. The soldier of experience is a stranger to monotony—he is part of a machine. All the comforts and amusements he can get outside of the routine life, are luxuries to be dissipated at a word of command.

Co. G dropped into the routine of camp life with good grace. They threw down brush upon the sacred soil of Virginia, they filled their ticks with dried grass, then spreading their blankets, composed themselves for the sleep of innocence, their knapsacks as pillows affording support to the shoulders galled in carrying them. Oh, those knapsacks. Sleep on, brave; bulge out knapsack, you are to be reconciled shortly.

Suddenly their dreams were broken—the day had dawned. From near and far came the bugle blast and the rattle of fife and drum. Hungry mules took up the refrain in varying keys. The boys of G soon heard the voice of Orderly Moore, "Co. G, fall in for roll-call!"

Drilling with the guns was for the first time attempted at Camp Chase and sergeants with tactics in hand, were drilling squads of men in all directions. A few lessons were given in the manual of arms by an officer of the regular army. As for Co. G, they forged ahead slowly, gradually cultivating a liking for a gun and accoutrements. They were drilled in squads, company and battalion evolutions, and rushed in this and that direction for health's sake.

The innocent verdancy of the sons of Lenox

was alike typical of all the companies. Officers made clumsy work with tactics and the colonel worked out his battalion evolutions quite gingerly. One day the regiment was marched nearly a half mile with arms at a shoulder, whereas they should have moved en route with arms at right shoulder-shift—a much more comfortable position.

The captain of Co. G at this time, was an emphatic, sharp spoken man, and sometimes his orders came red-hot and snapping. In one of the other companies the captain addressed his men as gentlemen,—"Gentlemen, attention to roll-call!" or, "Gentlemen, right dress, if you please!" Captain Beck, good man, had fitted himself, originally, for hotel keeping. Capt. Tuttle was a farmer. Beck's ways were very pleasant, but Tuttle's language and style were preferable even if he did embellish his orders occasionally, and surely he felt often provoked. For some men are always lagging behind, others never learn to handle a gun properly, and occasionally a man is found who never keeps step.

There were a few officers in the regiment who really used swear-words. Co. G was composed of a sterling set of mortals who knew very well that swearing was barred by Army Regulations, and Co. G knew better than to swear at an officer; yet, to swallow such bad treatment without mental comment, equally pungent, would have been unlike some of those sorely tried warriors.

But all this time Co. G men were bracing themselves for all emergencies. Physically, they were pretty hearty. They were learning to wash their clothing and sew on buttons and do a little patching, but they, as a rule were not supplied with Scriptural reading. So it came to pass that Gerrit Smith sent down bushels of small testaments to be distributed throughout the regiment as an inducement to the men to read the Scriptures. Into those beautiful knapsacks went Co. G's testaments. Alas, and alack, they were too generally allowed to remain there. A number of the boys could not read if they would, and more did not read, as they should. No evidence is at hand to prove that a man of Co. G ever caught a bullet in the testament carried in his pocket; and as they scorned to turn their backs to an enemy those testaments escaped a glorious perforation.

While on this subject a record should be made of the good people at home who were continually writing loving letters into which was lavishly insinuated a peculiar style of sermonizing, which though kindly intended and respectfully accepted, really did not accomplish much. They declared that the armies of the North were fighting God's battles; that the Lord would reward them. Over the rebel lines just such ideas were being instilled into the minds of Southrons. But Co. G, so wise were they, as not to charge the Heavenly Father of All with any denials that came to them. If they reasoned at all they understood, that, both North and South, it was the negro up the sleeve, or in the fence, that was causing all their misery. Indeed Co. G were more fighters than philosophers.

The donations of Hon. Gerrit Smith did not cease after sending the testaments. He also gave $500 to be used for the purpose of supplying the men of the regiment with stationery; a very thoughtful gift.

While at Camp Chase the troops were reviewed by Gen. Casey, when Co. G passed in review very satisfactory, to themselves; if the boys were not praised by others at this period in their history they could not very well understand the reason. They were not so green looking now, as they were getting sunburned and all of the same shade. The water of Virginia was not agreeing with all of them, but they were quite lively.

Army rations, particularly the bean and hominy, were gradually accepted as the proper food for warriors, and the company had some hearty feeders.

The locality known to Co. G as Camp Chase No. 1, was occupied about one week, when sanitary rules demanded a removal to fresh ground. Accordingly a site was selected in a field of scrub oak, which was cleared and the stumps grubbed from company streets. Such duty was called fatigue duty. Police duty, was the everyday work of policing the streets—cleaning up the camp. This duty was usually allotted to offenders, as a mild punishment, with the occasional addition of a chain fastened to a fellow's ankle to which was attached a small cannon ball. It must be recorded that Co. G. had a representative in the police gang at Camp Chase No. 2, who was wearing the ball and chain because of repeated disobedience. He was the first and the last of that noble band to thus disgrace the company.

At the new camp, excellent water was found. Fresh sweet soil made wholesome tent floors. As the camp was quite near the Lee mansion frequent strolls were enjoyed through the grounds and through the building. And for the first time, while encamped there, cartridges were issued and each man when equipped was carrying forty rounds. Soon after that event came a sensation that tried the metal of Co. G.

At two o'clock one dark morning the long-roll was sounded throughout the entire line. Starting a mile away, it came nearer and nearer, from camp to camp, until the band of the 157th struck up their drums. Buglers and drums, shouting officers and orderly sergeants startled the heroes into their respective company streets. Nor were the mules silent, mistaking the racket for an early reveille and call to feed. When the battalion was formed, the object of the alarm was met, and orders came promptly, to return the men to their quarters. That sort of drill occurred twice while the boys remained on Arlington Hights. The first time was frightful and some of the men were terribly shocked. But the second time they came forth promptly and becomingly. One year later the long-roll found them ready for anything, every pulse beating regularly and they were as calm as if on parade; for by that time they had become prime food for bullets.

Finally orders arrived to prepare for a march. The quartermaster had received his wagons and teams and among other accessions a sutler had located his tent near the camp, and was working up quite a trade in ginger snaps and green gingerbread.

Reveille sounded at 3 o'clock on the morning of October 12th. Tents were struck and with one day's cooked rations Co. G fell into line. About 7 o'clock the regiment started for Fairfax Court House, a distance of fifteen miles. Four hours consumed in striking tents, eating and getting away, was pretty easy soldiering; but they were learning a little all the time, those boys.

The road from Long Bridge to Fairfax had always been a long one for new regiments, and to Co. G, particularly so, on this march. Fifteen miles is not a great march for veterans. But heavy knapsacks, cartridge-boxes, haversacks and canteens and the rifle and bayonet, made quite a load for new troops. Co. G. started forth boldly in the misty rain and made their first acquaintance with the slippery Virginia mud. All went well for a few miles and then the column began to lengthen. Apparently the faster the colonel led the head, the slower moved the foot of the regiment, and when he reached Fairfax with the colors and a handful of men, the rear was but half way there. Brave Co. G. not to be out-straggled by the others, spread over as much of the country as possible, and when they drew near the town, Gen. Sigel was at the picket line to receive them. So interesting an occasion and one so novel was rare even in those days. The captain of Co. G, was at the camping place to receive them as they dragged in and reported themselves. And he spoke to them, cheerily, "Hurry now, and get the blank-blinkety-blank tents up. You have done blankety-blink well to-day, boys." Co. G knew all that and accepted the compliment. Stoical chaps, with aching shoulders.

One, and perhaps the greatest impediment to rapid marching that day, were the heavy knapsacks, although the cartridges, rations and canteens of water, weighed upon the shoulders of the boys with no kind results. But the knapsacks, crammed with necessary clothing, books, toilet articles, whetstones, hatchets, and much other stuff, three-fourths of which was dispensable, bore heaviest of all. All new regiments were similarly afflicted. Experience, however, taught in the army as at home.

Col. Brown, it is meet to record, was thoroughoughly disgusted with this first march of his men on a complete war-footing. Yet he was blameable. He should have known that forty pounds of regulation outfit was a full load, and that thirty pounds of additional weight in albums, revolvers and gim-cracks handicapped his heroes on the road. Even without sacrificing those stores of novelties, if the colonel had moved slowly, halting frequently and resting his men, he would have saved himself great humiliation. But he was getting schooled, learning something that he had overlooked or forgotten, at every public exhibition of his knowledge. He had called the men at Hamilton "my soldiers." One bright lad remarked "If he is our father, who in Hamilton is our mother?" He was indeed a fatherly sort of a man in some ways. As to their regimental mother, she never addressed her children, but was ever ready to enfold them within her bosom, and before three years had gone by, they became well acquainted with Mother Earth.

For some reason it was always harder on the boys marching under Col. Brown. Quite a contrast were Lt. Col. Arrowsmith and Major Carmichael, who were no less prompt than Brown; but they appeared to understand the men better. They realized that the short legged men were on the extreme left of the companies. That the tall men led the companies, and consequently unless all took the same length of step the line soon began to draw out; as on the historic march just mentioned.

The exercises at Fairfax resembled the ordinary routine, varied with exercises in firing blank cartridges. Men were here detailed for the first time for duty on outposts. A picket was stationed not far from the camp, who were given strict orders. With loaded pieces they stood post, rain or fair, in continual expectation of the arrival of the entire rebel army. No rebels appeared. Gen. Lee held no special grudge against Co. G.

While no rebels attacked Co. G at Fairfax there was another sort of gray-back came into camp. The colder weather of autumn and the dismal rains came on, adding greatly to the usual discomforts of tent life. Men began to sicken, others were homesick and consequently careless of their persons. Of course Co. G boys were mortified when the first specimens appeared and such a boiling of underwear as followed, checked the increase of the pest. The pediculus is in question.

Co. G were now being represented in the hospital. Sergeant Jarvis kept around as long as he was able, showing wonderful nerve, but finally was obliged to leave the company and never returned; being discharged, he was taken home by friends where with good nursing he recovered. In November, J. M. Ainsworth died in hospital at Washington, and Alfred Wilder died in hospital at Fairfax. Orderly Sergeant Moore was taken sick and left the company permanently.

So much sickness in the regiment suggested the need of better quarters and camp was changed. The men were ordered to build fire places and chimneys. An old building was sacrificed to supply bricks as well as lumber to use for flooring.

Fairfax was noted for many incidents worthy of note. Singular it was that so many of the boys cut their hands when procuring wood. In a few instances the forefinger of the right hand suffered. The surgeons became suspicious, after a while, for those accidents in most cases, appeared to be of an intentional character. The mania was not popular, the victims were not discharged. But ever after, such men were spoken of as those who were wounded at Fairfax. Co.G frowned upon such tricks so effectually that only one or two of its members caught the mania.

While at this camp the regiment was assigned to the 11th Corps under Gen. Franz Sigel, in the first brigade of the third division. Gen. Carl Schurz commanded the division and Gen. Alex. Schimmelpfennig, the brigade.

The 11th Corps was reviewed by Secretary Chase, at Fairfax, when Co. G marched proudly forth with expanded chests and flashing eyes to the brazen notes of "Hail to the Chief;" every one of them being a chief on his own mountain, he appeared to receive the music as a personal compliment; but after hearing it a few hundred times, later on, they leaned more fondly to "The Girl I Left Behind Me."

The 11th Army Corps was termed a German corps while in truth at least three-fifths of them were born in this country, and Poles, Hungarians, Scandinavians and Italians were to be found in the eleven so-called German regiments. Sigel had been praised for his good work at the Second Bull Run fight, and unfortunately being a German officer prejudice was aroused against him, and of course the corps commanded by him were considered "Dutch." It was a bad day for the North when Sigel was removed from that corps of willing fighters.

In Schimmelpfennig's brigade were the 74th Penna., 61st Ohio, 68th N. Y., 157th N. Y., and

82nd Ill., regiments, the last two new regiments. Sigel, Schurz,"Schimmel" and Col. Hecker of the 82d Ill. had all seen service in Germany and Hecker was one of the leading revolutionists there in 1848, in fact Hecker, Sigel and Schurz fled for refuge to America. Especially did Co. G feel honored to be placed in the division led by Carl Schurz, the patriot, statesman, gentleman and soldier. And so the brave Co. G were to go "marching on" with the "Dutch," but unfortunately never to fight "mit Sigel." They shared in the dangers of the 11th Corps. They shared in the severely unjust criticism the corps received.

The absence of ready means for trading purposes was beginning to be felt in Co. G. Now and then a fellow could produce a little money and was content. As the boys saw their money disappear into the sutler's till, they were said to then have bought pocket-books—as their cash was disappearing they began to save, like true soldiers; and when the last dollar was gone they regretted their foolishness, like all the world. They were at school and in the freshman year; shortly, the sutlers will have a story to tell.

Money of the war was greenbacks and postal currency in fractional parts of a dollar. As soon as the war began the speculators hoarded the silver and the people were soon obliged to use the bills of state banks, and shinplasters issued for fifty, twenty-five and ten cents, by merchants and others, redeemable at their places of business. Ordinary postage stamps were circulating in small amounts enclosed in diminutive envelopes and passed around as change. So when Co. G went to the front such of the boys as had bills on state banks, found them useless. And the tormenting postage stamps were often found stuck together from the perspiration of one's body. Although mustered for pay Co. G had not yet seen a paymaster. So they drew on funds at home, if they had any, and in traffic received the beautiful new 50s, 25s, 10s, 5s and 3-cent paper currency; an event worthy of remark. The greenback came out late in 1861, and McClellan's men and others received them who previously were paid in gold.

A sad accident occurred while the company was at Fairfax. It was on a pleasant day, October 30th. The boys were at platoon drill when they were interrupted and returned to camp. One of their comrades had been shot. His name was Henry Richardson, who being detailed on fatigue duty was at work arranging for a hospital tent.

A detail from the 26th Wisconsin regiment returning from picket duty, had discharged their guns into an embankment a half mile distant and in line with the 157th. A stray ball went over the bank and struck Richardson on the side of the head, killing him instantly. There was not a great deal of mirth in camp the evening following the accident. And when the bright moon came up, a line was quietly formed and followed the ambulance down the road to the picket line, the fifes and muffled drums playing the march for the dead. Members of the regiment had subscribed money and the body was taken to Washington by Sergeants Hemstreet and Gates, there embalmed and forwarded to Canastota. And for a long time, the deep shadows of the oaks, the white cover of the ambulance and slow stepping body of men who marched to the solemn music, was an impressive scene and one seldom commented upon. In the language of one of the boys, "It was bad enough to be shot at by rebels," without additional risks from the rifles of their friends.

In the latter part of October orders came to pack up the superfluous clothing, which included of course albums, quarto dictionaries, library books of all kinds, hardware, etc., already toted so far in the knapsacks. The object was not so much to lighten the loads of the men as to increase their speed. Gen. Sigel had not forgotten that memorable march from Arlington in which Co. G succeeded so well in lagging behind. And so it happened that a cart load of boxes filled with the surplus wardrobes and toilet articles and bric-a-brac of Co. G. were stored somewhere in Fairfax and to be left there as prey for looters.

The first day of November marching orders came and the boys took the road for Centerville. At one of the first resting places the knapsacks began to drop and in their place the popular blanket roll was hung over the right shoulder, thus supplying a nice pad for the rifle to rest upon while marching. The same scene of disburdening occurred at every halt, until the men were reduced to easy marching order, and at every halt the ground was littered with the goods. Germans following who were better fitted for the task, loaded themselves like pack horses; and what the Germans did not take was culled over by the teamsters. What cared Co. G, their shoulders were now relieved.

The first day's march was through Centerville and down the hill to Bull Run, encamping near

Stone Bridge, a locality noted for the scene of slaughter there but a few months previous. Coffee was boiled in turbid water from the stream and the boys bivouaced under the stars. The boys of Co. G thought hard and rapid that night as they gathered like frogs along the margin of the stream and bathed the pouching blisters which adorned their heels. No matter what they thought of other matters, the men of G were never known to lack in respect for one of those old army blisters; and the more the blisters smarted, the more they were respected.

Co. G were tired and even the snorers of the company were quiet. There was Jerome Forbes a capital snorer; he was soon promoted to a lieutenancy and probably then gave up snoring. And Hub Suits who bunked with Jerome, was an excellent second. But they all slept quietly that night for those fields were reminders of serious conflict. Around them lay a good-sized army, victims of two great battles: lay as fallen soldiers are buried on the battlefield, in shallow trenches or above the ground with a thin cover of earth over them; their fleshless skeletons protuding to mock the so-called glory in war. And only the stars looked down compassionately. Those sleeping forms of the living also were offerings, and of the 157th, every ninth man was to be lain on the nation's altar before the close of the war. Still they slept on, perhaps dreaming of home, of mothers, wives, babes. What a miserable trade is war?

It was on that terrible field the chaplain of the regiment received the acceptance of his resignation. He was a good man,—had served the gospel but little to the men. He declared later, that he was discouraged. He never did any harm, if he did no good. Co. G were very sorry to lose the chaplain, for they felt the dignity of the regiment was well guarded so long as a man of peace was with them. No, no, Co. G had done nothing to discourage the chaplain; possibly he was shocked by those long-rolls on Arlington Hights. —But the bugle sounds the reveille.

"It appears to me people are in the habit of rising early in this part of the country," remarked Doc White, as he gazed upward into the constellated arch.

"Yes," spoke John Miller, "and I must carry that grist to mill to-day."

"You'll carry it on your back, Miller," called out another, in memory of a knapsack.

"Co. G, fall in for roll-call!" sang out the orderly sergeant.

The line of march this day lay toward Thoroughfare Gap. Not far from Hay Market the column halted and were drawn up in double-column on the center.

"Attention-n-n!" yelled Col. Brown. "My men, the enemy are supposed to be near. They have been seen to-day. You may shortly be called into action and I expect every man to do his duty. Remember, the eyes of Cortland and Madison counties are upon you. Attention! By division, right wheel! For-w-a-r-d, March!"

Off into a field and skirting the woods, moved Co. G. Another wheel and to the left, and the advance began. They moved briskly and steadily along, until one of those narrow wash-outs peculiar to Virginia soil, yawned fully four feet in width before them. Over went the divisions like sheep, the major in the lead, for alas, the horse ridden by the colonel—the old cow—refused to take the ditch. Fortunately the eyes of Madison county were not present at the circus which followed. Thump! thump! went the colonel's heels against the ribs of the cow; then he whirled and dashed at the obstacle again.

All the time Co. G were on a still hunt for wandering rebels. And when the colonel, by making a wide detour, succeeded in overtaking his men, they were well across the field and had not bagged a single johnny. The company generously shared their disappointment with Colonel Brown, just the same as though he had kept his place with the column. The colonel had been foiled—and that, his first Virginia ditch. In fact that was not a day really rich with glory for Madison and Cortland counties.

As the field manoeuvre was over, the column again took the road—it was doubtful if there was a force of rebels within twenty-five miles.

Toward night Thoroughfare Gap (an opening through the Bull Run mountains) was reached and Co. G bivouaced in the oak woods with an abundance of leaves for bedding. Two nights they slept on the ground without tents—no great hardship in good weather; but the second day at the Gap the shelter or dog-tents arrived; the day following they were pitched, after a fashion.

While at the Gap the entire division of Gen. Schurz appeared to have run wild. Every house, the fields, all property was exposed to the looting soldiers, who were well supplied with government rations but craved chickens, fresh mutton and tender beef, honey, home-made bread, jams, and jellies. The camp of the 157th resembled a market. Cattle and sheep were lowing and bleating in pens, fowls were plenty and dressed carcasses, hams and many other articles and things hung from the trees. Guns were popping and stray bullets flying, for the brave boys had discovered the presence of the saw-back hog, a species common in the South, usually running at large. They had first met him on the road while marching in, when the big saw-back with long snout to the ground claimed the middle of the road, and got it too; going down from the head of the regiment to the rear, the ranks opening graciously to allow him to pass. And he minded little the bayonet jags pushed at him as he sped as only his family can run. But many a saw-back fell that day, of all ages, from roaster to patriarch.

After some hours of such ill-becoming looting, strict orders were issued and guards thrown out about the camps. A few hours later the doctors were busy with sick men who had gorged on honey and fresh pork.

Thoroughfare Gap witnessed several contests during the war and many times the cavalry, either of yanks or johnnies, saw each other's heels flying through that winding defile with warm spurs. And the place was remembered ever after in the annals of Co. G, as the camp where much property was stolen and also the locality where Dan Brockway left his little leather-covered trunk.

Dan was formerly a peddler of various kinds of flavoring extracts, ink and bluing. For some funny reason he carried a stock of his essences with him into the army; a strange freak indeed. He had lugged that package thus far, patiently bearing the compliments of officers and men as they urged him to keep in place. He was one of the smallest men in the company, but it took one of the largest and the strongest to land him on his back at square-hold. Brock was always good natured and always busy.

The day came for another moving and the captain said in a firm, but pleasant, way,

"Brock, you must get rid of that blinkity-blim box of yours. Do you understand me?"

Brock understood, as when the captain spoke that way he was in earnest. So the box of beautiful extracts, cinnamon, peppermint and the rest, was left at a house near the gap and is there still, perhaps, for Co. G never saw it again.

The 11th Corps had been thrown forward to guard the supplies for McClellan's army then on the march from Harper's Ferry. Large quantities of stores came up and were in waiting for the advancing columns, and as soon as the Army of the Potomac had gone into camp near Warrenton the 11th Corps was moved to New Baltimore.

Orders for marching came Nov. 7th, a chilly, cloudy day. Before the march of twelve or fourteen miles was half concluded, snow began to fall and Co. G pitched their tents at New Baltimore, in a brisk snow storm, and in a cornfield. Corn stalks were plenty and served for tent-flooring. It was a blundering piece of work, ordering men to camp in a muddy cornfield while a few rods distant was a desirable rise of ground, to which they were removed within a few days. The 157th had many experiences among corn stubble, until the boys came to counting upon such a bivouac as sure whenever one was found conveniently at hand. Blame was unjustly attached to Col. Brown for those cornfield camps.

The continued bad weather caused much sickness among new troops, and consequently the army was weakened. McClellan advised going into winter quarters, but the Northern press howled, "On to Richmond!" and the administration removed McClellan and placed Burnside at the head of the army.

The troops were drawn up to bid farewell to Little Mac. His progress could have been traced by the cheering of the men. McClellan was popular with the rank and file of the Potomac army. Had his advice been taken and a vigorous campaign opened in the spring, thousands of brave men might not have fallen in vain, with other thousands of sick besides, not to mention the heavy losses in stores and equipments. Those campaigns conducted to gratify a clamoring press were not popular after Gen. Grant took command of the Army of the Potomac. As soon as Gen. Burnside was well established in his new command he began his move on Fredericksburg.

At New Baltimore the regiment was for the first time joined by the lieutenant colonel, Geo. Arrowsmith. Col. Arrowsmith had seen considerable service and when the regiment was organized his name was pressed for the colonelcy over his former tutor, Brown. The appearance of the lieutenant colonel was pleasing. He was a tall, strongly-built man, his face was pleasant and his voice was clear and strong. The men enjoyed being under his command, because there was an air of confidence about him not possessed by the inexperienced officers. There was no hesitation when Arrowsmith gave an order, for he gave none new to the men without first explaining and making it clear. At Fairfax, Brown had captains and even sergeants attempt to evolute the battalion, while he kept one hand on the machine that it might not blow up. But Arrowsmith had none of that nonsense, and for some reason it ceased soon after he came.

November, 1862, was very trying for the people at home as well as the soldiers in the field. The election of Horatio Seymour as governor, encouraged the Peace Party. At the front was Burnside surrounded by officers and men antagonistic to him, who growled at his appointment and criticized his every move. The malcontents among the corps commanders favored McClellan and if not he, they wished to have some one beside Burnside, who was a good man, and all he lacked to make his plan successful, was hearty co-operation among his subordinates.

As already stated the men were growing more sickly. The hospitals were filled and many were ailing in their tents. Co. G, amid all the misery and the growling and incipient disloyalty, remained steadfastly loyal. Its heroes marched up and took their quinine, or they marched away to picket-duty. But they were being thinned out and details came heavier and heavier upon those who remained well. The principal malady was dysentery, which weakened the men quickly, but being of a mild type in most cases, there were few fatalities.

The return was begun Nov. 17th over soft roads, slippery with mud, made worse by the rain which began to fall about noontime. After dark the men bivouaced in a field of corn-stubble, rain falling and small rivulets running down between the rows. The boys were served with boiled potatoes, warm from the kettle and graced and blessed by Billy Mallows, the cook, who growled and snarled while he cooked, until the very potatoes rolled their eyes at him. Thankful was he that night that he was soon to leave the emblazoned service, as he soon after did to give place to one of the best company cooks in the regiment.

At this cornfield camp near Gainesville, a

whisky ration was served to the men. They had fixed their bayonets and driven them into the ground, strapping a third gun across for a ridge-pole on which to lay their tents; then spreading a rubber blanket on the wet ground they made their beds for the night; a bad arrangement in case of alarm and against orders, but they could do no better in the dark.

So the heroes turned-in, their heads on one corn row and their feet over another, their bodies sort of zigzagged-like, in the form of a letter Z. There they lay dreaming while the rills of muddy water coursed under them, poor Co. G, until aroused by reveille. Then they turned out, stiff and uncomfortable, but otherwise not in bad shape. Col. Brown was very temperate, and whiskey was never issued unless the occasion was urgent, and this was one of those occasions and the first one—no doubt it was timely.

Marching was difficult on the route to Centerville, Nov. 18th, and led over another portion of the Bull Run battlefield some distance from Stone Bridge. For a long way the ground was littered with relics, and then Brock proceeded to load himself down with bullets, grape shot, etc., in spite of the remonstrances of the officers, carrying into camp twenty or thirty pounds of lead and iron. He was thinking of the money in such pickings. For a long time after, he amused himself whittling the bullets into axes, hatchets or hammers duly handled in red cedar, which he sold when possible as souvenirs to be sent home by mail. For Brock had a family and in any way he could earn a penny, was sure to make the most of his opportunities, sending the money home. And he was temperate as he was saving.

Camp at Centerville was made on the bleakest part of the hill near the little hamlet; not far from where, the preceding winter, the enemy had built large-sized barracks. Those rebel huts were torn down and the wood used to construct shanties for the newcomers. Winter set in and the cold winds whistled across the bleak hill most wickedly.

Reasons for army movements sometimes are based on pure assumption. And such reasoning may have worked out a plan by which the 11th Corps must remain at Centerville; but a hill should have been selected broad enough to receive the entire corps, headquarters and all. Such disposition of the troops might have been made as to place them nearer wood and water, and so reduce exposures and lessen such large attendance at surgeons' call. While commissioned officers must not find fault, they must obey offensive orders emanating from superiors.

Occasionally there is a little discretionary power allowed an officer. When the vacant huts were apportioned to the men one came to the share of Co. G. Then it happened that the men of another regiment undertook to appropriate Co. G's share. Down came Capt. Tuttle loaded for large game, and the Captain of the strange men was there also. The interview between the captains was short and very emphatic, resulting in G securing the timber. On another similar occasion on the Gettysburg march, when the regiment went into bivouac they were told to appropriate all the rails in their immediate front. Shortly appeared a mob from another regiment who were bent upon carrying away those particular rails. The intruders were scarcely at work when Col. Arrowsmith rode among them revolver in hand. The 157th boys gathered their rails at leisure. The boys felt that it was good to have their officers interested in the comfort of the men.

There were a few of the companies in the regiment very much neglected that first winter out. The men were good material and in time became as good soldiers as any in the command. The first lieutenant of one of those companies insisted that his captain was dead and should be so informed. But the captain did not believe it, and proved the contrary, when he showed enough life in him to resign and go home.

Near the camp at Centerville resided a shoemaker, Pettit, by name, and his wife and three grown daughters. A houseguard of one man from Co. G was stationed there to protect the premises from looters. The family treated the guard kindly and also admitted a number of sick boys who rapidly regained their health as soon as removed from the exposures of camp.

There were but one or two attempts at drilling while at Centerville and then under advice of the doctors as for physical exercise. One day the troops were marched to Chantilly and exercised in a mock battle.

Just as soon as Burnside was well set down in front of Fredericksburg he wanted the 11th Corps and of course, Co. G. Then came a tedious march.

December 10th, after a tramp through snow and mud a distance of five miles, the troops bivouaced at Poorhouse Station. The night was cold. A canteen of water placed under one man's head was found frozen nearly solid in the morning.

Next day's march was eight or ten miles across Wolf Run Shoals Co. G going into bivouac in a dense pine thicket on the hights beyond. No tents were raised, some pine boughs were thrown upon the frozen ground and with feet to a cozy fire the boys slept the sleep of the weary.

The marching on the 12th was very bad. The weather had moderated and the bottom fell out of the roads. That mud of Virginia is peculiarly tenacious and quite frequently a fellow's shoe was pulled from his foot. Before Dumfries was reached misty rain was falling, which soon rendered the roads in some places impassable for heavy wagons or artillery. So it was necessary to call a halt until the wagon train was brought in, and men were detailed to pull with the mules whenever necessary.

Two nights at Dumfries rested Co. G and the boys started onward to the aid of Burnside's men, whose cannon were distinctly heard fifteen or twenty miles away. The corps reached Falmouth the day following the departure from Dumfries, or Dec. 15th.

The 11th Corps was promptly prepared to be ready for crossing the Rappahannock next morning. Guns were cleaned and arms and ammunition inspected and the loyal G expected to be ordered into action. Fortunately for them and for humanity generally Burnside decided that enough brave men had been sacrificed. There was a report that Sigel had passed condemnation upon the hopeless plan of that battle. Certainly history has done so time and again. The ifs and other remote contingencies did not warrant such a terrible sacrifice. The certainty of failure was apparent after the first day's fighting. The only hope was in flanking Lee, which failed.

To hold their own was too easy for the rebels. An artillery sergeant told the writer, that the section to which he belonged bore directly upon the flank of the union troops, as they charged Marye's Hights, and he pitied the brave fellows who again and again charged forward only to be swept away.

"Sir, I was sickened at the sight," said the rebel sergeant, "I dreaded to see them moving up without the slightest chance of success. The ground in range of our guns was covered with slaughtered men."

It was just as well for Co. G that the needs of the nation did not call them to charge those deadly hights. They were after glory but preferred it not quite so hot, and even had they won a fair installment of glory it would have been denied them. Seldom is that battle mentioned now. Great stories are told of Pickett's charge at Gettysburg, however, almost as famous and as hopeless as that of the six hundred at Balaklava—all brave men but needlessly slaughtered. Why should not Burnside's men at Fredericksburg be remembered with equal pride?

Men may decorate themselves with all the glitter of rank and strut with dignity through street and camp, and yet fail to prove themselves worthy of a command in time of great need. But the subordinate and the private soldier has but one way of showing his importance—strict obedience to orders from those above him, no matter whether the officer be a man or a manikin.

Co. G enlisted to do, or to die trying. They read newspapers and knew that Gen. Patterson failed to support McDowell at Bull Run; and the sacrifice of Col. Baker at Ball's Bluff by the neglect of Gen. Stone; the neglect of Sumner to support Heintzelman at Williamsburg; and that Fitz John Porter failed to succor Pope at the second battle of Bull Run. Co. G understood a number of things, and they gazed upon big general officers with awe. They had narrowly escaped the slaughter, but shared in the humiliation of the hour; feeling more comfortable, however, than did Gen. Burnside, who knew that the blunders were not all his own. Co. G were ready to support Burnside, to a man.

On the 17th of December the 11th Corps turned back from the Rappahannock and camped near Stafford Court House, traveling in a brisk snow storm over very soft roads. On the 18th they moved to a fine piece of timber some distance from Stafford and proceeded to build a permanent camp. Other troops occupied the ground before Co. G came, and had begun the work of laying up log huts.

In a few days the camp was quite habitable— with shelter tents for roofs, stone for fire-places and chimneys, laid in mud, with an occasional topping off with barrels. Co. G terraced the sloping ground where they made their beds, and were careful to keep their heads level. They cut the boughs of red cedar and laid them deep above the damp earth. The fire-places smoked inside as well as out, by the use of green oak for fuel, and the little dwellings, in fact, were considerably tainted thereby with an odor akin to that of soap-boiling, an abiding fragrance; and the eyes of the heroes were moist with tears while the oak was frying. Very wrong indeed it was, to throw blank cartridges down a fellow's chimney; and such capers were cut up in some of the companies, but not in G, who were dignified. The honor of Lenox rested, the easterly portion upon the shoulders of Co. B, with Co. G at the other end, and they carried it from their homes to the depths of Florida, and brought it back untarnished; unless critics wish to bring up chickens and such—but chickens do not count in affairs of honor.

For the first time since leaving Hamilton Co. G were short of rations. Hardtack was scarce for a while at Stafford and the thought itself is hungrifying. Piteous reports reached their homes and the good people there filled boxes with food and other comforts. And one day, soon after the holidays, the regimental teams brought in a car-load or two of boxes, long delayed on the road, and the abundance of army rations for a time, were neglected for better fare. To those fellows who received no boxes, was freely given by the more fortunate. In many instances the boxes were found rifled of much of the original contents,—a common occurrence. There were gangs of plunderers hanging about all army depots and landing-places, who were ever waiting for opportunities, and they would steal the food from the sick, rifle knapsacks of the living and the pockets of the dead, whenever possible. Many of those depraved creatures were enlisted men, and those of them who lived long enough, no doubt, became pensioners; consequently, heroic veterans. Yet Co. G were glad if the boxes only came, seeing in them lumber for small tables or doors.

The holidays were passed in this camp, with Col. Arrowsmith in command. Brown had been furloughed. A few of the boys were lucky to obtain fowls and hoe-cake, from the residents living near. In some of the squads they parched corn obtained of the teamsters, or battery-men. Money was very scarce and there was a tobacco famine. The poker-players used bills of broken banks and bills advertising Morgan's rifled cannon, or some business college. They had been mustered, but not paid.

One day a stray sutler stopped at the camp. He was a pleasant man and the boys patronized him freely, until the merchant discovered he was exchanging his goods for worthless paper. Col. Arrowsmith was appealed to, with no satisfaction, and the sutler moved along, sadly.

After that, for a time, tobacco was plenty in the camp. Those who had been smoking coffee or chewing a stick, now were willing to prosecute the war in earnest. The ginger-bread eaters were lively as crickets, but the stock of bad money was low.

At Stafford there were frequent desertions among the men. Several left the good society of Co. G. The men were discouraged like the chaplain, and many of them would have resigned were it not that they thus would desert their officers.

The officers of the regiment were getting discouraged also, some of them because they were homesick, some because they were better off at home, and many because they were sickened of warfare. They had marched over one hundred miles, saw the smoke of a terrible battle, and their ardor was appeased. By the middle of January sixteen of them had resigned from discouragement and one from disability. Twelve left at one time, and later on others resigned, until Capt. Frank Place of Co. C, was the only one left of the original ten captains and he returned with the regiment as major. His first lieutenant, J. A. Coffin, after serving a long term in rebel prisons, returned and was mustered out as captain of that company. Captain Dunbar died, of disease, Capt. Adams of wounds, Captains Frank and Backus were killed in battle and Capt. Stone died in prison at Macon. Thus accounting for the original thirty line officers. In spite of such terrible temptation, Co. G were true. "Guide North!" exclaimed one of the departing captains, as he mounted a baggage wagon; and quite a number of his men soon followed him. Similar changes were going on in all of the new regiments.

Sickness prevailed alarmingly at Stafford. A crowd of men attended surgeon's call each morning and kept three doctors busy until long into the night. Fortunately the serious cases were comparatively few. The illness resulted from exposures and the inexperience of the men, in most of the cases.

For the information of any persons who are ignorant as to knowledge of the shelter-tent it may be said that this kind of a tent is used by troops in the field in active service. Each soldier draws one piece of tent,—a piece of white or unbleached twilled cotton cloth about one yard and a half square. In two corners of the cloth are loops of light rope to be used when the tent is held to the ground with stakes; around the margins of three sides of the cloth are button-holes set at regular distances, and two inches above each hole is a bone button. As they are exactly alike, any two soldiers may join their pieces and thus raise a shelter, or three or four, by uniting and pitching the tent at a right angle, can close the tent ends, using two of the pieces cornerwise. Buttoning together the pieces for roofing only, they could be extended to any length, and sometimes, by exercising a little ingenuity, they were made to cover quite a large building. Thus is space devoted to this subject because the shelter tent was an important article in the outfit of Co. G.

What is called the Mud March began January 20th, 1863, when the Army of the Potomac was ordered out of their snug huts and started on a campaign against the enemy.

Before daylight on the 20th, Co. G were routed out and ordered to strike tents and take the road. Old Ziba had cooked beef and pork and the boys carried, also, three day's rations of coffee, sugar and hard-tack.

Lieut. Bailey had been transferred to Co. K, as captain, Lieut. Frank was promoted in Bailey's place and Sergeant Hemstreet was made second lieutenant of Co. G.

That particular morning Capt. Tuttle was not in very good humor and the boys of Co. G were hustled around lively; and they were all ready and waiting in good season, for the order to move.

They had quite a tramp of ten or twelve miles, halting at Hartwood Church, near night. Soon rain began to fall and at dark was coming down quite briskly.

A pontoon train that was drawn up waiting for the arrival of Co. G and the other troops, as soon as darkness came on, started for the Rappahannock river a few miles distant, where engineers were to lay a bridge, that in the small hours of the night Co. G (with other troops) could be slipped over there quietly and as the daylight returned the astonished rebels were to find they had work cut out for them. Unfortunately, the rain softened the roads and the wagons bearing the pontoon boats stuck fast in the mud. The artillery that was to cover the laying of the bridge also stuck in the mud, and horses and mules stuck in the mud. And it became necessary to send men with ropes to pull the wagons, artillery, horses and mules out of the mud.

When scouts of the Union army approached the river next day they saw a board duly lettered with these words—

"Burnside Stuck in the Mud."

Co. G had been kept in suspense expecting momentarily to be ordered away, until word came to the boys to make themselves comfortable as possible. A picket was thrown out near the camp. But the failure of the expedition brought little comfort to those unfortunates who were obliged to stand out two hours in the cold rain, which poured from their caps down their back bones and into the shoes. Sleep to a weary soldier is sweeter when he knows his faithful comrades are watching over him, particularly on such a stormy night.

Burnside had again been unfortunate, this time doing just enough to christen his effort with a most appropriate name, "The Mud March," and it appeared to the army that the elements had conspired to save them from another defeat. Lee was prepared for the event and his guns were placed to sweep the bridge if laid.

Burnside pulled and lugged until he had the greater portion of his army back in their old quarters near Falmouth.

The 11th Corps went into camp on Oakland Farms in a handsome piece of timber. Chestnut trees supplied material for huts and the men were soon busy.

While in this camp snow fell to a depth of one foot. The demands for details for picket came often—the lines were heavy. The rebels were known to be near.

How fiercely the wind swept the light snow in blinding eddies around a fellow's head those nights, compelling him to trot lively or freeze. Posts were relieved every hour instead of every two as was usual. At the grand guard below the hill, in the woods, a bright fire was kept burning. When relieved from his post the picket made his bed on two rails propped above the pools of water and melting snow. Such experiences were common in bad weather.

The army shoes were the greatest hindrance to comfort. They were made of leather poorly tanned, and frequently brown paper was found laid in between the outer and inner soles. Such affairs soon wetted through. The consciences of army contractors were terribly warped during the war time. How very wicked it is to tempt some men with fat contracts.

When the shanties were nearly completed, Feb. 5th, orders came to move nearer the base of supplies. Co. G were getting familiar with house-warming and moving-days. Already had they built three shanties and were now to pack up and journey into a new country and raise a fourth. Such experiences were not pleasant in the depths of a Virginia winter.

An unpleasant march through mud and snow brought the men to Potomac Creek where they stopped for the night. Next day they reached Accokick Creek and were marched into a dense growth of pine favorably located on sloping ground, and about three-fourths of a mile from Brooks Station.

Col. Brown ordered the men to build huts and arrange for a stay of months. Many of the little buildings were really comfortable. When the regiment moved into the wood the timber stood very dense but not large. A few days later not a tree was standing; all had been cut down and converted into building timber. Stone was scarce and many of the huts had fire-places of wood well plastered with clay, the chimneys of sticks laid up in clay.

Once more were the boys of Co. G settled in house-keeping and ready for company. It was a pleasant camp in many respects. The health of the men improved, food was abundant, good water convenient, plenty of picket duty, very little drilling, mail regular; a sutler was adopted by the regiment, and finally came a paymaster, and Co. G were happy. This was the first time they received pay after being in the service, nearly six months. The sutler gave credit, however and thus had a tobacco famine been averted.

Paymasters are generally well received among troops. Many of the men had left at home dependent ones who needed relief. But in most instances the money was not really necessary. To be sure money was needed for postage but that was about all. Ginger-snaps, canned lobster and oysters, or jelly, and hair oil were better on the shelves of the sutler's tent. Sardines might also be listed, inasmuch as two of the boys of Co. G were punished for stealing sardines from a sutler.

Co. G were not out to inculcate morality, and felt the shame of detection in any case in which their honesty was involved with a sutler. They were modest men. Hugh O'Brien was shocked when he heard that those boys had been betrayed by one of the company who had partaken of the stolen sardines; and Hugh reached forward quickly and struck the informer, because he had "peached" on the boys. Hugh was too good a soldier to be severely punished.

While in this camp, Capt. Tuttle resigned and Lieut. Frank was made Captain. Hemstreet was promoted to first and Sergt. Gates second lieutenant, and John H. Roe to orderly sergeant. Co. G supplied officers on short notice to other companies if required and retained plenty of material made up and anxious.

During those dreary winter days, while the fate of the nation was undecided and the newspapers were wiping from the face of the earth the last trace of rebellion, fathers and mothers grew very anxious for their dear boys at the front. Some of them wrote fault-finding letters, deploring the war. The majority, however, never for one moment doubted the result. And the dear girls, how loyal they were. So tender and true. They were worth one hundred thousand men.

"Say, Mamie," wrote a comrade to his sister, "do you know that Dick actually kissed the last letter you sent him? I really believe he is licking the stamp this very minute."

"Please write me no more such nonsense as that, Sammy dear," she replied, "as I do not believe you. If true, Dick would soon suspect me devoted to the filthy habit of chewing tobacco. Father affixed that stamp."

Frequently a letter came from some fair one, a total stranger to the soldier; for the girls felt they were justified in waiving formalities, while risking censure from cynical people. Their letters were very acceptable. Nothing did more to hold the boys within the bounds of morality and decency than the kind letters from home. Many of them have preserved those pages, creased, crumpled and worn and to their last days will regard them as the choicest relics of the war-time.

While at the camp among the stumps, Col. Brown inaugurated his school for commissioned officers. Many of them needed schooling. It was reported that an examining Board had been instituted at headquarters.

The colonel also gave instruction to the non-commissioned officers, and privates who yearned for advancement.

Added to his other beneficient undertakings, Col. Brown regularly conducted prayer-meetings at his quarters. He had been a missionary teacher among the Choctaw Indians and likely supposed the 157th offered fruitful ground. If the colonel had stopped there, he would have done better. Soon a chaplain appeared.

United States Army Regulations provided that "the wishes and wants of the soldiers of the regiment shall be allowed their full and due weight in making the selection" of a chaplain. What use could Co. G make of a chaplain. They were enlisted in war. Their plowshares and their pruning hooks were far away in Lenox among the hop-vines, "up the creek," and they carried no swords.

What need had the regiment or the army for a preacher? Why not have a regimental lawyer? Only in rare instances was a chaplain worth the salt he ate. In garrison a preacher may be useful as a school teacher, but he is not needed in active service. Co. G had believers and skeptics,—Protestants and Catholics—to have forced a chaplain upon that company would have compromised their sacred rights and liberties. They were "fighting God's battles," and every one had a nice little testament, somewhere.

Co. G were not allowed their "full and due weight" in the matter of a chaplain. As a man there was not great fault found with this chaplain, and he held forth acceptably. He was only one of thousands of supernumeraries who could well have been dispensed with, in that trying war.

In his General Order No. 1, of Jan. 27, 1863, Gen. Hooker says, "He enters upon the charge of the duties imposed by his trust with a just appreciation of their responsibility."

Gen. Burnside in his final order relinquishing the command of the army to Hooker, says "Give to the brave and skilful general who has long been identified with your organization and who is now to command you, your full and cordial support and cooperation and you will deserve success."

Burnside commanded the army about eleven weeks. Hooker, about five months.

When Meade superseded him. Hooker in his farewell order says, "Impressed with the belief that my usefulness as the commander of the Army of the Potomac is impaired. I part from it, yet not without the deepest emotion."

By comparing the sentiments expressed in those extracts one would imagine that Burnside had reason to feel consoled when his successor failed.

The real, real key to all the troubles experienced by Gen. Burnside will be found in the letter of President Lincoln to Hooker when he tendered the command to him. It is a characteristic production of Mr. Lincoln, in which Hooker is severely rebuked. Never has the full extent of the criticisms against and neglects practiced upon Burnside, been exposed to the public. But from the tone of the President's letter one would infer that Gen. Hooker was not considered blameless.

This much of history and comment is given because the gallant Co. G are soon to meet the enemy and win laurels under Joe Hooker, which are never accorded them.

Early in 1863 Gen. Sigel was superseded by Gen. O. O. Howard as commander of the 11th Corps. The badge of the 11th Army Corps was a blue crescent on a white field. Funny fellows in other corps declared it was a "flying half-moon." Co. G cared very little for such flings. As for "flying," they knew the records of many other corps, and they also remembered Sigel had been highly praised once upon a time.

With Co. G the world kept rolling on, and after the proclamation of emancipation it really looked as though oil had been poured in at the axes. The patriotic order or address issued by Gen. Schurz on Washington's birthday, brought up the shades of the past, and Co. G seemed marching on, in sunshine, escorted by the fathers of the revolution. The signs were declared to be favorable once more.

Gen. Hooker, to cheer up the army, granted ten-day furloughs; two men were to go from each company, and when they returned, more were furloughed. The first two from Co. G came back promptly. Of the next, but one returned, consequently Co. G could have no more home-going. The scamp who deserted was always troublesome. He had been detached at division headquarters. How he ever was allowed to step between good, dutiful soldiers and the prospect of furloughs, is not known. The fellow was discovered as a bounty-jumper, at Elmira a few months later, and courtmartialed, and sent to Fort Clinch, Florida, to complete his term at building fortifications.

As spring approached and the ground became

firm, the men were drilled regularly. Inspections were frequent. The Sunday morning inspection related to cleanliness of person as well as arms, equipments and quarters. Every man was obliged to stand at "attention" with one foot bared, and occasionally the surgeons ordered prompt bathing. A very few of the boys were taken by a guard, to the creek and there scrubbed. Co. G. had none of its members forcibly bathed, but a fellow occasionally would escape with one clean foot. By and by, whenever possible, the men were cleanly for sake of comfort.

When Sunday inspections came the cook-houses were thoroughly looked after. Ziba Cloyes the cook of Co. G and Pat Matthews, his assistant, kept all their kettles and pans in first-class order. Nobody needed fear to partake of Ziba's fare. He was an old hotel keeper and understood culinary matters.

Ziba's violin was a great exhilarator and the boys gathered around his tent to hear the well-known strains of good old-fashioned reels and hornpipes played, in style. And they straightway paired and whirled in stag-dances, stepping to the strains of Ziba's music.

When Gen. Hooker took command of the

army he reviewed the 11th Corps. Gen. Howard also reviewed them. And a review, to soldiers in the field, often forecasts a movement of the force.

Gen. Schimmelpfennig had the brigade out for drill. Col. Brown frequently marched the regiment out for new manoeuvres, and Col. Arrowsmith did the same. Capt. Frank had Co. G drilling for the first time as skirmishers, a drill which was of little use unless accompanied by actual, genuine experiences.

On the 10th day of April, 1863, the Army of the Potomac was reviewed by President Lincoln. Co. G came out in fine feather. New uniforms and blackened leathers, polished brass, clean guns, and white gloves. The boys were fast becoming useful soldiers. Discipline had greatly improved their appearance; drill made them prompt and correct.

When the boys marched past the President in company front—"Eyes right!" came from Capt. Frank—there sat, upon his horse, a plain citizen, who bared his head and smiled as though he knew every one of Co. G and could name them all. The line was fine, their carriage good, and Capt. Frank was proud of his men. It was a red-letter day for the company.

Capt. Frank seldom made speeches. That day was an exception. When the company returned to camp, the captain said—

"Boys, you have done well—you have done nobly—as well as any of them. You have done bully, by ginger! Orderly, break ranks."

During the latter part of April orders were received to pack all superfluous clothing and send the boxes to the river. By this time the supply of books, albums and the like, was exhausted. Much of more value to a soldier, had accumulated during the winter and Co. G made a fair showing of packages. Those goods were never returned to the men.

Spring weather had come and the little frogs and the big frogs were telling the world of it. Trees were beginning to leaf out and grass was showing here and there. Hooker thought it time to make a move.

On the morning of April 27th with eight days' rations and sixty rounds of cartridges the men left their huts and started for Chancellorsville—of course their destiny was unknown at the time, but Co. G scented the battle from afar. The haversacks were filled with hard bread, boiled beef and pork, coffee and sugar. In the new knapsacks were surplus rations and twenty rounds of cartridges. No trouble now with knapsacks, for the load was light; but the haversacks dragged upon a fellow's shoulder. There was this consoling in such a load, it kept growing lighter and lighter, each meal.

The boys felt well and marched along in fine style. Co. G were becoming weather-beaten and seasoned.

After an easy march the column halted beyond Hartford church for the night. Next morning was rainy. During the day the troops were moved up near the Rappahannock and marched into the woods and told to keep very quiet and wait until it was dark.

Toward midnight Co. G, with the others, were moved down to Kellys Ford. The pontoon bridge was covered with earth, men were forbidden to speak aloud; a move to flank the rebels was in progress.

The 157th was the first new regiment to cross over. In the ranks of Co. G strict silence was enjoined. Charley Near was not permitted to torment Pete Cummings. A truce was established, temporarily, between the Johnsons, Zerne and Jim. Ir Sayles was not singing. Orderly Forbes marched at the front supported by John Pfleiger and Amos Avery, while Dan Brockway brought up the rear. Dan always led the company when they marched left in front. All was quiet. The boys declared the night was so dark they might bite it; but the report that the pioneers went ahead and tunneled a passage through was pure imagination.

After crossing the river and ascending the slope a faint line of light could be traced along the horizon. The regiment was marched to its position in line of battle and halted, to await the arrival of other troops, and later were moved forward to a piece of woods and went into bivouac.

Early the morning of the 29th, rebel cavalrymen were seen in the distance and a few artillery shots were thrown at them. Col. Brown rode forward to reconnoiter, soon returning hotly chased by the naughty johnnies.

The route taken that day was toward the Rapidan. Late in the afternoon the column arrived in the vicinity of Germania and lay until after night, waiting for a bridge to be laid, for the enemy had destroyed the crossing. When all was ready, Co. G marched down to the river. A narrow passage had been prepared, by laying planks from one abutment to another, down close to the rapid flowing water. Large fires were burning on either bank to light the way. Co. G went over, cautiously, without wetting a foot. John Schultz had resigned; had he been present, it is likely he would have turned turtle, the same as he plumped into the slip at New York. But the entire corps got over safely and went into bivouac on the cold, wet ground. No fires were allowed until daylight.

The halt after crossing the Rapidan is known in the annals of Co. G as the time and place where Brock was detailed to guard the fiddle of Ziba, the cook.

Now the boys were to march in the enemy's country. Before crossing at Kellys Ford, the regiment was drawn up and reminded that the eyes of Cortland and Madison counties were upon them, which was no news to the heroes. Col. Brown's tone on such occasions sounded very solemn as though the eyes of those counties were sad.

The boys respected Col. Brown; they could not blame him for not showing a cheerfulness he did not possess. There was something about those speeches suggestive of a lack of confidence; it is believed the one delivered at Kellys Ford was the last of the series. Col. Arrowsmith never commanded the boys in battle. The methods of Col. Carmichael will appear as the record develops.

April 30th opened misty and unpleasant. The road passed into the celebrated Wilderness, finally striking the Fredericksburg plank road. In the afternoon the destination of the 11th Corps was reached, and the men were bivouaced nearly in position for battle.

May 1st the historic order congratulating the right wing of the army was read to the men. "That the enemy must either ingloriously fly, or come out from behind his defenses and give us battle on our own ground." He came, he saw, and the result is history.

The troops were ordered to burn all clothing and prepare for light-marching order. The Army of the Potomac was preparing for a lively race toward Richmond. Such an order proved wise and timely, and much was destroyed that otherwise would have fallen into the hands of the enemy.

Towards night the 157th was moved forward nearer the plank road and ordered to strike arms and rest. Appearances favored a fight. Soon after dark a rebel battery threw some shells over the line and Co. G, for the first time heard the bang! pop! whi-z-z! of shelling; no one was struck. But few shells were thrown, when all was quiet again. Johnny reb. was only feeling for Co. G.

Many of the boys long remembered the whip-poor-will chorus in the woods about them, as they lay behind their guns that night. When the rebels opened fire the birds ceased at once. The enemy had spoiled the concert.

May 2d was Saturday. Fresh beef was issued to the men about noon time, and the company cooks proceeded to arrange their kettles for boiling the meat.

All this time Stonewall Jackson is approaching Hooker's right flank. Several officers from the picket line came in and reported to headquarters of Howard, that the enemy were working around on the right. Maj. Carmichael, of the 157th, was on the line; he was one of the brigade officers-of-the-day. Those officers by message and in person informed the commander of the 11th Corps that the enemy were moving in force.

Says Maj. Carmichael, "All these messages received the reply that we were green troops more scared than hurt."

About the time the officers from the picket line were trying to arouse Gen. Howard to action, Gen. Hooker sent him these instructions:

"The disposition you have made of your corps has been with a view to a front attack by the enemy. If he should throw himself upon your flank he [Hooker] wishes you to examine the ground and determine upon the position you will take.* * * He suggests that you have heavy reserves well in hand to meet this contingency. * * * We have good reason to suppose that the enemy is moving on our right. Please advance your pickets * * * in order to obtain timely information of their approach."

Howard's headquarters were lethargic; his troops were enjoying themselves.

Stonewall Jackson was a very busy man while Howard was reclining very comfortably at Dowdall's Tavern.

While the events just related were occurring the boys of Co. G were writing letters which the chaplain was to carry away and mail. One of those letters, written on a drum-head, portrays a scene as follows:

"Nearly all the privates in Co. G are on picket. It is a novel sight to see the men, who are in good spirits, taking their ease. Some chatting, some cooking, others playing cards, while many are writing: but the most of them are sleeping."

It was about this time that Jackson was conducted to a knoll overlooking the position of Howard's men. He saw the whole display of neglect—the absence of supporting columns and all. And he started his men forward.

Near five o'clock p. m. the storm broke. First a few shots and then a volley. From the extreme right came rushing a crowd of supernumeraries of all grades. Thirty thousand rebels had surprised the first division of the 11th Corps. A portion of the first and also of the third divisions were absent reconnoitering. Back came the first division upon the third, followed by the exultant enemy. The boys of the first division did all they could, but what could they do?

Col. Brown was ordered forward and then countermarched to a position east of the Hawkins house and behind some shallow rifle-pits thrown up the night before. Gen.

Schimmelpfennig says, reporting to Gen. Schurz—

"The first line of our division in connection with Col. Bushbeck's brigade of Gen. Steinwehr's (2d) division, formed behind two of our regiments, the 82d Illinois and the 157th N. Y., (the first commanded by Col. Hecker and the second by Col. Brown) and occupied the rifle-pits. * * * Your two brigades and that of Col. Bushbeck, together comprising not quite 4,000 muskets, alone received the entire shock of the battle and held the enemy in check at least an hour. The three brigades above-named although both their flanks were turned, stood their ground until a sufficient time had elapsed for the other corps to come to their assistance and take position in their rear.* * * For the surprise on the flank and rear, in broad daylight, by a force outnumbering us four to one, the responsibility falls not on the third division. * * * General, I am an old soldier. Up to this time I have been proud of commanding the brave men of this brigade; but I am convinced if the infamous lies uttered about us are not retracted and satisfaction given, their good will and soldierly spirit will be broken."

Good, brave "little Schimmel," their soldierly

spirit was not broken, and they were yours to lead for many a weary mile through stifling dust and burning heat.

The battle of Chancellorsville has gone into history and may be found therein by any person who wishes to follow the battle. So far as Co. G are responsible, little more need be said.

After the terrible experience near the Hawkins house, the 157th was withdrawn in excellent order and retreated, after some delay, to the rear of the newly formed line of battle. Adjutant McWilliams was dispatched in the gathering gloom, to find the proper road, and went straight into the rebel lines, and was forwarded to Richmond. Fortunately, the opposite direction was taken, and Col. Brown led his men safely out of the woods. They lay in reserve on Sunday and Sunday night, when the artillery of both forces shook the ground and filled the air with bursting shells. Early in the morning of May 5th the Army of the Potomac was withdrawn and in a miserable rainstorm dragged themselves across the Rappahannock and paddled through the mud back to their old camp on Accokick Creek. When they marched away they took the road— on their return they came across lots and found much easier traveling.

There was an important part played by Battery I, 1st Ohio Artillery, in the Chancellorsville fight that adds to the record of Schimmel's brigade, very much. Capt. Dilger, a Prussian officer, who commanded the battery faced the advancing men of Jackson until nearly cut off, losing one gun. He then retreated down the plank road. Sending four of his guns to the rear he retreated leisurely, firing as he went and clearing the enemy from the road.

But the gallantry of the boys of the 11th Corps was overlooked in the general casting of results. There must of course always be a scape-goat for blunders in war, and it would not have done to place the blame upon West Point graduates.

The losses of the 157th regiment in the battle of Chancellorsville fight, aggregated about one hundred. Co. G lost, Asa Lawrence, killed; John Pfleiger badly wounded and Henry Whaling slightly wounded,—the least number hit of any company in the regiment. Co. A lost the most men in that battle—one lieutenant and three men killed and sixteen men wounded and missing. Co. B came next, with three men killed and ten wounded.

It was sad to think, after computing the fatalities and speculating upon the fate of the missing, that away up in Lenox the people were reading in the newspapers that Co. G were not so great a success, after all. That their dear boys had "marched up the hill," exchanged shots "and then marched down again." As communities, would Clockville, Hoboken, Wampsville and Canastota have preferred to see their sons brought home on their shields rather than had Hooker made a failure? Perhaps so. Very likely. But Co. G were satisfied to live just as long as possible.

Nor did the galling tirades of War Critics cease with the passing of the moment. Before the War Committee of Congress, and in standard history, the bile of the enemies of the 11th Corps is spread the mark of Cain. Many of those critics are now dead, but their works do follow them. No Corps of the Army is so bitter in comment of this kind as the 1st Corps, and they did not reach the field until after Jackson was checked. Then there was still time to win laurels, fresh and brilliant. Ah, the world will never knew why the corps did not come up in time to help Co. G whip the naughty Jackson.

One of the missing of Co. G was Dan Brockway, the bodyguard for Ziba's violin. A few days passed and the news came that Brock was a prisoner. But he was promptly exchanged and was soon present at roll-call.

"Brock, how about the violin?" asked one.

"Well it was this way, boys. I was in the tent, when the rebs came and told me to crawl out. They sent me to the rear."

"And the fi-f-f-fiddle," asked John Miller. "T-t-tell us about the—here—here—f-fiddle."

"Oh, I carried the fiddle with me. By and by along came a reb and wanted to borrow the thing. I told him it belonged to Ziba, and I didn't like to part with it. 'Oh,' says the johnny, 'I'll take good care of your fiddle; there's a right smart of we'uns can play.' So I let him take it, and he never brought it back."

"I'll tell you what, b-boys, we oughter do. Jest take the b-blamed little cuss over there and exchange him for the here—here—fiddle. What do you say, boys—hey?"

It was a dreary reception the boys found on their return to their old shanties. Rain was falling and the interiors of the huts were thoroughly soaked. But they stretched once more their tent covering and moved in. Fires were started and fresh boughs laid upon the bunks, so it was not long before everyone was comfortable and the routine of camp once more established.

Then came fresh soft bread again and other food, denied to a campaigner. The sutler returned from his retreat to safe quarters. He had learned the tricks of the men and they had learned something of him. He was not a bad man, by any means. Occasionally a hole was cut in his tent, and canned food and tobacco disappeared from right under his eyes. In such matters of course, Co. G had very little to say.

There were a few boys in the company who were sharp in dealing with sutlers. They were pleasant comrades and did their duty, but if opportunity presented, they were not slow to act. One of them, usually was well supplied with fried pies, and pies sowed and pegged (suggestive of boot leather. This boy if asked how he obtained his truck, replied, "Oh, I coddled them." Poor boy, he fell at Gettysburg—a good soldier on duty, but a terror to sutlers.

There was another diversion upon which the pious element of Co. G frowned—poker playing. Col. Brown prohibited gambling. It was a still night and a dark one, when there was not a game of poker going on. And at "taps," which brought the officer-of-the-day around to see that all lights were out, blanket screens were arranged so that the light did not show through the tent roof. The click-clank of a sword as the officer approached, caused the light to disappear, and sure to be relighted as soon as expedient. With their caps between their knees, the candle propped up in a bayonet, and a hard-tack box for a table, they whispered back and forth and shuffled and dealt until some of those caps were filled with postal currency. But poker was not the only game played in the tents—euchre was a standard game.

Soon after the return from Chancellorsville the winter camp was abandoned, for sanitary reasons. Added to accumulated foulness nearer by, the half-buried corpses of a number of mules and horses out beyond the parade ground, were beginning to pollute the air.

The place had been home to the boys. Its associations to many were pleasant, to others, saddening. One of Co. G's boys had died while there and was buried in the little enclosure back of the camp. His name was Foltz. The suggeons said he died of home-sickness. His friends soon after removed the body.

But camp must be changed. Precisely as with some people renting houses, it is more convennient to move frequently, if they can thus avoid house-cleaning. Thus was it with the 157th, and a summer camp was established on Greens Farms, not for from the old one.

The new camp was neatly arranged, tents raised from the ground, company streets turnpiked and adorned with evergreens, and at the head of each street was an arch bearing the company letter in cedar sprigs. Fine water gushed from beneath a huge gum tree below the hill, supplies of all kinds were abundant and the men of Co. G kept in health.

The wounded from Chancellorsville were brought over and placed in tents not far away, conveniently near for visiting. John Pfleiger, wounded below the knee, suffered from a painful wound. Hank Whaling was grazed below the stomach with a piece of shell. He had but recently recovered from an attack of measles when he went into the fight, and his voice had left him, so that he spoke in whispers. When he was struck, the shock restored his voice, and he yelled, "Hub, —— —— I'm hit!" He finally recovered from the effects of the bruise, and saw more of the war.

When money is plenty among soldiers in camp there are always traders of various kinds on hand. A maker of tin-types set up his shop nearby and drew quite a trade. Some of those old pictures are still in existence and they are fondly treasured. Occasionally a proud son of Lenox borrowed the coat of an officer to appear smart in the picture he was to send to his deary. By far the greater number appeared before the camera rough and unpolished; sometimes in blouses, with pipes in their mouths, and caps tilted on their heads. Not at all like the frozen figures of Hamilton days.

One result of the recent battle was the depletion of the color-guard. While at dress-parade one evening Col. Brown delivered one of his measured speeches.

"Men are needed to fill out the color-guard," he said. "Candidates for vacancies can send in their names to the adjutant. I want none but brave men. The post is one of great danger. The appointment means promotion."

A subdued growl went down the line, for the speech was a commentary. Brave men! Just one man in Co. G sent in his name, and he did it to avoid guard duty. A few weeks later and a private soldier of Co. G carries the flag off a bloody battlefield. Where were those brave corporals? The sergeant was down, several of the corporals were wounded. The brave color corporal from Co. G was scratched and left the field with all its glory behind him and he never returned to the company.

One beautiful day the battalion was taken out for a drill in charging. Col. Arrowsmith commanded half the men and Major Carmichael the others. The boys were moved about, here and there, until at last they started over a sharp knoll and the divisions met, with bayonets fixed at a charge and the officers and men cheering. Company A's captain and the lieutenant commanding B, crossed swords and the fire flew for a few moments. Both were quite warm over the matter. The voice of Col. Arrowsmith stopped the threatening storm. It is safe to say, neither of those swords ever again came so near drawing blood. For the officers' swords in the infantry, usually, were applied to switching off the tops of grass and daisies, or killing snakes; few of them ever tasted gore.

Dress swords were issued to the orderly sergeants and to duty sergeants also. They were carried only for a short time. One or two campaigns and superfluous equipments disappear.

Usually, their rifles were sufficient for the boys of Co. G. Those nice little swords would have answered for toasters when sharpened sticks were scarce.

In the first weeks of June orders came for the men to be supplied with extra rations and eighty rounds of cartridges. Gen. Hooker intended the men should carry plenty of powder and ball.

Sick and wounded were sent away, and with the sick went Lieut. Hemstreet, who had resigned. The sutler also struck his tent and followed after the man of the picture gallery, seeking a quiet, out of the way place.

Even the men who peddled the Washington newspapers (for ten cents, which cost them but two and a half cents) they, too, flitted.

The ins and outs and the ifs and wherefores of those days are mystifying literature. In the North the so-called Peace Party were seeking by every means in their power to bring the war to a close. That party had but recently in a convention held in New York, declared "That under the Constitution there is no power in the Federal Government to coerce the states, or any number of them by military force."

Horace Greeley compared those resolutions to the fourteen reasons offered by an Irishman in court, as to why his father was not present. The judge decided on hearing the first one—that the father was dead and couldn't come—was conclusive, and waived the remaining thirteen.

So amid the jangle of peace in the presence of war, on June 12th, the 157th moved out and marched to Hartwood church. A short rest at Potomac Creek was made memorable by a generous donation of cigars by Col. Arrowsmith, who was temporarily in command. Col. Brown was detached for a day or two and led a brigade of the first division.

The march, June 13th, was nineteen miles in a hot sun, over dusty roads. The men suffered greatly that day and were glad when Catlett Station was reached.

Co. G pitched their shelters, dug small trenches under the drip of the tents and prepared for a wet night, for the sky looked very black, the air was hot and lightning was playing in the distance. Camp was made in a heavy growth of young timber where plenty of fuel was found, coffee was made and the weary sons of Lenox turned in, tired, tired.

When the storm broke the much quoted and yet ever fearful Virginia lightning flashed out spitefully, thunder boomed and the rain came down very heavily. Amidst the racket an occasional shout was heard from some person who had failed to provide for bad weather—"My roof leaks!" or "the cellar of my house is afloat!"—ordinary occurrences.

The march on the 14th was eighteen miles, across the Manassas Plains to Centerville and camp was made near the old camp ground of the preceding winter.

The corps rested at Centerville two days, lying in readiness for a battle. And a rest was needed. Such extreme hot weather began to tell upon the men. Many of them were suffering from blistered feet; and a few men had been overcome by the heat.

On the 17th of June Co. G were again on the road, at night stopping in a sheltered hollow by the waters of Goose Creek.

This day's march of but seventeen miles, was exceedingly severe. Dust rolled up, filling the eyes, penetrating nostrils, and even the mouths of the men. They were thirsty, but the steady, close-file marching made it lively work for the boy who fell-out for water. The guns were loaded and flankers thrown out and uncertainty and discomfort appeared on every hand. Toward noon, a bend in the road led down between two thick fields of timber. The dust seemed finer and lighter than ever, and the rays of the sun darted down into that oven of a place, most viciously. Suddenly the regiment opened right and left, other regiments did the same, the men staggering into the fence corners, everything looking blue and misty before them; while a thumping noise sounded in their ears.

Directly the boys heard the voice of "Little Schimmel," who appeared to have been in the rear, as officers were marching left in front. Forward he came, shouting—

"Halt the column! Mine Gott, what for they kill all my men? Halt the column!"

Soon the general came back, cheering up the boys with a promise of coffee in the shade. Co. G rallied and found, just ahead, the shady grove. An hour's rest, and they were again ready for the road.

As they filed down into a cosy camping place by the creek that night, the men resembled the gray-back johnny rebs, more than they did boys-in-blue. They resembled men who had been rolling in the dust. However, it was not long before Goose Creek was thoroughly appropriated for bathing purposes.

While the gallant G are resting at Goose Creek, in a camp located on elevated ground, the good people at home are worrying about them. Lee's advance-guard has been seen in various places across the Potomac. A force of rebels have pressed into Pennsylvania and the whole north is excited. One hundred thousand militia from Pennsylvania, Maryland, West Virginia and Ohio, and twenty thousand from New York have been ordered to Harrisburg. All the troops about Washington have been placed under orders. The greatest anxiety exists as to Lee's point of attack.

Vallandigham has been tried for seditious utterances and is to be sent over the lines to his Confederate friends. The party clamoring for peace is unceasing in their efforts. But the great heart of the loyal North is true.

Lee, it came about, had great hopes that this effort would be of practical worth to the cause of secession. The Confederate government hoped his success would benefit their cause abroad. And with a united South and a divided North, the rebels were to come out, ultimately, with honor. Such was the hour of preparation, of anxiety and of hope.

On June 21st heavy cannonading was heard in the direction of Aldie, and Howard's corps were placed under waiting orders, but they did not move.

Co. G were taking the world very comfortably, eating dew berries and milk and saving up strength for the next grand movement in the programme.

June 25th quite a number of convalescent men returned to the regiment from the hospitals at Washington. Among them was Durell Moore, a boy of Co. G. All of those boys looked rather pale for vigorous campaigning.

"Jerome," said Durell, as the orderly handed him a gun and accoutrements, "these things will be the death of me." It was a thoughtless remark lightly spoken but one that was noted. He was the first man (so said) in the company, killed at Gettysburg.

The afternoon of the 25th camp was broken and the corps moved down to Edwards Ferry, on the Potomac, and bivouaced in a fine field of clover. Engineers were out on the river laying a bridge and the noise of moving teams and falling planks lasted long into the night. Co. G had now become convinced that the whole weight of the contract did not rest upon them, and content and sleepy, too, they lay among the clover blossoms on the hillside, their feet to the river and their faces turned toward "God's country." They gazed at the North star and talked of home. Then sweet sleep came.

Early on the 26th the corps began crossing over the bridge of boats. A bridge laid under the supervision of Capt. C. B. Reese of the Engineers, a Canastota boy.

As the head of the regiment struck Maryland soil the boys cheered. They sang "John Brown's Body," until the chorus rolled from the end of the line. Then was heard the old hymn, "We're Going Home to Die no More." Alas, yes—nearly one out of six of them was to be left dead at Gettysburg, and scores of them writhing in pain.

They were in a new country. Virginia's neglected acres gave way to fields of corn and waving wheat yellow and nearly ready for harvest.

Monocacy was passed and the column filed through a narrow gorge and took the road to

Jeffersonville. The boys of G felt well and indulged in much nonsense, similar to this—

"When are you going to cut your wheat, Steve?" inquires Doc White.

"I expect to begin the first of the week," replies Harrington.

"Orderly," says Zerne to Jim Johnson, "I think I see a rebel at that house over yonder. You will take Loucks and Wise and surround them."

"—— —— —— ——!" from Jim.

And so they moved along. Think kindly of them, reader; they are rough, but their hearts are right. They have followed a tedious road for many miles to fight for Lenox, for humanity—South and North—to save the Union and free the Negroes. The little part they have in the great drama entitles them to recognition, and to a mite of sympathy.

Rain set in toward night making the roads slippery. Plenty of new-mown hay was at hand, also good, seasoned rails in abundance. Maryland farmers grumbled some at such wanton destruction. It was a Union officer who pointed to his empty sleeve and said to the complaining farmer—

"Your crops will grow again, your woods will supply you with rails. This sleeve will always remain empty."

Starting out on a cloudy morning, the 27th, the column passed through Jeffersonville; the brigade band stationed by the roadside treated the boys to a little cheering music.

Reaching the streets of the small town Co. G were excited to see here and there a handkerchief waved to them. Out of the ranks sprang one of the boys.

"Come back here, what are you doing?" called out several.

"Nothing great—only wondering how it seems to walk on a sidewalk."

Near night they reached Middletown. The band unlimbered and went into action, the boys straightened up and kept step. Ladies waved flags and little boys shouted. Quite a number of houses kept closed blinds, which very likely opened when the boys-in-gray marched past and then other blinds were closed.

Beyond the town camp was made in a region ripe with dry rails and fresh hay. It was at this bivouac where Col. Arrowsmith interposed for his men as already stated.

Next day, June 28th, was Sunday and the church bells rang. Co. G were called up and formally notified that Gen. Hooker was satisfied Gen. Lee and his army had crossed into Maryland.

"You will reduce yourselves to light-marching order. Those who have blankets will tear them in two," said the captain.

Light marching order! Indeed, very little remained to be sacrificed. Many of the boys were reduced to the last shirt, To lighten up a few ounces, nearly every man went to a convenient brook and a crowd of them were soon busy, bathing and washing that last shirt. Long before those garments were dry, a headquarters bugler sounded the "Assembly." Clutching their washing from the bushes, the boys hastened to camp and were soon on the road again; some of them vainly trying to dry their shirts by throwing them over their knapsacks and tying the sleeves under their chins, thus gathering more dust than before washing. And the shirts went into the ditch.

It was a short march to Frederick, which was reached early. A delegation of small boys were out to meet Co. G, and as they marched around the outskirts of the town the rail fence was lined with little boys and girls, the boys on the top rail gazing at the free show. At one point where the children were collected, a tempting rail-full of all colors came in view.

"See the little—here—here—r—rebs! Doc," exclaimed one to his neighbor.

"Get back into the ranks, Loucks!" called out a half dozen. "You wouldn't hurt a child, would you?"

"I believe in taking them when they are young," growled Lute Loucks, one of the kindest-hearted of boys.

He had jumped toward the children with his rifle clubbed. Of course the ridiculous caper raised a laugh, in which the children joined merrily. Those jolly fellows were the life of the march.

There was Al Bridge, his face always prepared for a smile, his ways were pleasant and his heart was light. Jim Travis and Dan Grovestein skylarking all day on the road and going into camp at night kicking up their heels. Charley Ricker, another young boy who appeared too frail for the road, yet tough as whit-leather; Hugh O'Brien, with his stories of the fairy order, or of his experiences along the Erie Canal; Nick Ecker, not much of a talker, but a loud laugher, and others who trudged along enjoying the fun. They were a good crowd to be with, kind to each other. Rarely were angry words heard among them.

In fact, the entire regiment enjoyed an excellent record for good order. At times the camps of some of their neighbors were very noisy, especially when they were having a high old time; but that sort of thing was not permitted in the 157th and if ever it did occur, it was conducted in a manner worthy of the occasion.

Gen. Hooker had asked to be relieved and Gen. Meade took command of the Army on June 28th, 1863, at Frederick, Maryland.

When the 11th Corps filed out into the road on the morning of June 29th, they opened ranks to let Gen. Meade and staff pass; the boys were braced up for loud cheering and waving of caps, but the general took a different route and Co. G moved along on the Taneytown road, just enough rain falling to keep the road "greasy," as the men said. But a good long march was made and Emmettsburg was reached before night, the troops camping near the town.

The morning of the 30th, Schurz's division

were moved near the town. The quarters of the 157th were on grounds adjacent to the Convent of St. Mary's. It was an unpleasant day. There were many changes being made by the new general.

The 11th Corps was passed by the 1st Corps at Emmettsburg and went into camp a half mile distant. Gen. Reynolds of the 1st Corps ranked Gen. Howard. Had the 11th Corps been thrown forward, instead of the 1st Corps, perhaps they would have made as fair a showing as the 1st Corps on the pages of history. They certainly were as good men as there were in the army.

Pickets were detailed from the company while lying at Emmettsburg. When the boys returned to camp, they were well supplied with home-made bread and other good things.

Wednesday, July 1st, the 11th Corps resumed the route to Gettysburg. Before the column is ordered to move, a glance along the lines of the 157th will be interesting.

The regiment left Hamilton something like nine months before, with over eight hundred men. Now they are drawn up in line and number three hundred and eighty-six muskets. Reports have been given of their sufferings from sickness and in the Chancellorsville fight, and desertions, which have combined to reduce the regiment to the present figures.

They have been pictured as cleanly, well-dressed men. Now they appear neglected. Their clothes show hard service, the shoes, especially important, are getting hard wear. Rapid marching and lightening of knapsacks has reduced the boys' underwear; few of them have but the one shirt, which is in use. That big chap in Co. C is unable to hide, with his blouse, the fact that he has sacrificed his last shirt for the cause. But they are the boys of Cortland and Madison and even though they are out in the rain and the mud, their pulses are regular, and their powder is dry.

The corps moved leisurely along the Taneytown road until near noon. At Marsh Creek, Battery I passed the regiment, its support. Soon after, heavy canonading was heard and orders came to double-quick the men.

For two miles or more the fast walking and trotting was kept up until the boys drew near Gettysburg. They had come about twelve miles, and were approaching the town from the southwest.

On the hills beyond and west of the village, the 1st Corps were hotly engaged. Citizens were met coming from their homes in the town, in some instances laden with light articles. They were frightened. No wonder.

As the boys went through the streets men and women were gathered in little groups here and there, with pails of water, which the boys gratefully swallowed and hastened along.

Outside the town and north and east of the Pennsylvania College, between the Carlisle and Mummasburgh roads, Battery I was already in position and ready for work. The 157th was stationed in rear and to the right of the battery, near the Carlisle road, in a small field of growing corn.

A rebel battery took position a half mile distant and opened on Battery I. Shells came rapidly, pieces struck among the 157th quite freely. The faster came the shells the more Co. G hugged the soft earth. That sort of thing continued for a time, until Capt. Dilger had dismounted several of the rebel guns, when the others were limbered up and driven to a new position. In the meantime one of the corporals of the color-guard was killed and a lieutenant was wounded in the hand.

An order came to Col. Brown to advance his men. They started forward in double-column on the center and—to use the colonel's expression—with "alacrity."

"Battalion, halt!" somebody yelled.

The batterymen were shouting and Co. G were wondering why they were being taken through a battery while it was firing.

"About, face!"

And they returned and moved to the left of the battery and then forward down the slope, the boys of Battery I firing over their heads.

Proceeding forward two hundred yards, the regiment deployed in line of battle. A line of rebel skirmishers were coming over the rise in their front. The rebs to the number of fifty or so, threw down their guns and came forward and surrendered. Several men were detailed to take the prisoners to the rear.

Off on the right, skirmishers were very busy. Shells were flying toward them from two rebel batteries.

"Battalion, double-column on the center— March! Right wheel!"

Then it was, under lively shelling, those much-abused fellows quarter-wheeled to the right, as steadily as if on their quiet parade ground.

Again they went forward and over a rail fence, into a field of wheat standing ready for the reaper. Then came the order to deploy column.

"Co. G, not a man of you fire until you reach the line, and then give them a volley!" shouted Capt. Frank.

The boys had met the enemy again and some of them were falling. Peter Agan, the first man hit in the company, fell with a ball through his thigh. Another man fell forward and bellowed like a calf and as the company went forward he crawled to the rear and deserted—unhurt.

Into line went Co. G. They formed on the colors, steadily and ready.

"Co. G, give it to 'em!" called out the captain and a grand volley was sent toward the line of rebel heads which were bobbing up and down over the wheat, twenty rods distant. Then the fighting began. It was murderous while it lasted—only about twenty minutes.

At one time Col. Brown ordered a charge and the line surged forward for a few rods. Again they halted and stood up for a time and took their medicine like men, giving back their best.

Along that line the boys were falling in all shapes. Then some one shouted "get down into the wheat!" And thus was the fighting continued in Indian fashion. Zip! zip! came the bullets, scattering about the ripe wheat wastefully.

"What did you-uns stand up like that for, and be shot down?" asked a reb of one of Co. G's boys, a prisoner.

Capt. Frank, Capt. Backus, Capt. Adams and Capt. Briggs were down—the two former, killed. Other line officers were killed or wounded. The gallant Lieut.-Col. Arrowsmith was dead. It was a question of but a few moments when his entire regiment would be disposed of, and the colonel looked about wistfully for an approaching aide.

A staff officer finally came riding rapidly toward the field. He reached the line of fire and his horse fell. It was Capt. Klincker of "Schimmel's" staff. Klincker dismounted, waved his hand to Col. Brown, then unfastened his saddle and with it started for the rear.

Col. Brown ordered a retreat. The scattered remnant of his regiment, their organization broken, a sorry sight, left the field.

Joe Hart, of Co. G, as the order came for retreat, arose from the wheat. Near him lay the colors. He picked them up and started for the rear. He succeeded in reaching the fence, when he was shot through the leg. Joe tossed the flag over the fence to Ir Sayles of G, who carried it from the field.

Col. Brown rallied his men near the town, and a few shots were fired, and then continued their retreat.

Capt. Frank was killed, Lieut. Gates badly wounded, Co. G had lost nearly one-half its numbers and the few still on an army footing were exceedingly lonesome.

The streets of the town were soon blocked with ambulances, horsemen and men afoot. The exulting rebs were pouring into town in steady pursuit. Batteries from a distance were sending shells after the retreating Yankees. It was no time to stop and visit.

"Little Schimmel" remained too long to look after his men and nearly was captured. As he spurred away his horse was shot. The general sprang into a side street, which proved to be a cul de sac. He climbed a fence and found himself in the garden of Henry Garlach. The rebels were rapidly spreading over the town, and escape by the street was impossible. He espied the Garlach woodshed. Near the outer door stood a swill-barrel, and back of that was wood, cut for the stove. "Schimmel" was a small man. He cleared a space behind the barrel, where he secreted himself by piling wood about him. There was a small peep-hole through the wood and when Mrs. Garlach came into the shed, the general whispered to her, told her he was a Union officer and begged her not to betray him. Rebels were going through the houses searching for Union soldiers. They entered the wood-shed even. Although she was terribly anxious lest the rebs should find a soldier secreted on the premises, Mrs. Garlach did not forget that the general might be hungry. Her son was a lad of ten or twelve years, and she whispered to him aside, then handing him a large pail in the bottom of which rested a cup of water and some bread, she said aloud for the benefit of some rebel soldiers in the house—

"James, take this pail to the shed and get some swill for the pigs."

The boy successfully passed the food to the general, which was all he had for sixty hours.

July 4th, when the Union troops reentered the town "Schimmel" came forth, mighty stiff, but otherwise in fair condition. And when his old regiment found him they wept; they hugged and kissed the little man; better pleased than if he had been killed and buried ten feet deep in honors. They believed he had been taken prisoner.

When Orderly Forbes gathered in all the could find of Co. G, he had about a dozen men. (The word "about" is used because there were a few detached men). The corps was once more in position on Cemetery Hill. The 157th remnant lay with the reserve on the site of the present National Cemetery. And lay they did, on July 2d, and very flat. The rebels had concentrated their artillery fire upon that part of the line.

Just at dusk this reserve was ordered out on the right. The men were ready. The 157th followed the 61st Ohio, a veteran regiment; together they numbered less than one hundred men. By some mistake the 157th party became divided, a portion following Col. Brown and the others, Capt. Place. It was a night without a moon, and in the shadowing woods, very dark.

Just as the 61st and the detachment of the 157th under Capt. Place, "had reached the angle of our line," writes that gentleman, "a volley was fired from behind a stone wall in the edge of the wood....the woods beyond were all ablaze with musketry.......several of the detachment were killed or wounded. The officer commanding the 61st ordered his men to file to the right and left as fast as they could. Our men were ordered to follow. When out of range the boys were halted and it was then discovered the colors were missing." The color-bearer, Geo. H. Davis, of Co. A, had been wounded.

Capt. Place felt, as soldiers should feel, at such a time. And the eyes of Cortland and Madison were upon them. Believing that they had been fired upon by Union troops, Captain Place, with privates Marcus Livingstone of Co. C, and Francis M. Gault of Co. G, went back to find the flag, but they found that the rebels had advanced their lines, and they were soon prisoners.

Once more did Co. G try to score a point for the old flag. One of their boys had brought it from the deadly wheatfield, and was wounded. Another had volunteered to accompany the gallant Place, and was captured. Gault had a taste of rebel prisons from Richmond to Andersonville, returning to the company in April, 1865.

On July 3d the remnant of the 157th, then pretty well banged-up, were withdrawn from the front and placed on provost duty at the quarters occupied by Gen. Schurz.

The first roll-call after the battle occurred the evening following. Thirty-nine privates, eight corporals and four sergeants answered to their names. The entire regiment, July 2d, consisted of Col. Brown, Major Carmichael, Captain Place of Co. C, Lieuts. Jenkins of Co. B and Tallman of K, and fifty-six men. Other officers were present at the time of the fight, but were not acting with the regiment.

Out on the wheatfield lay Col. Arrowsmith, Captains Backus and Frank and Lieut. Lower, while thirty-three enlisted men, dead, marked the regimental alignment. Capts. Adams and Briggs, Adjutant Heenye, Lieuts. Smith, Waters, Gates, Atwater and Fitch, and acting lieutenants Harrington and Benjamin, wounded. Of enlisted men more than two hundred were wounded, some of them slightly, many severely. Two officers and twenty-one men died of wounds, making casuality list foot nearly two hundred and sixty men, and fifteen officers.

Capts. Stone, Place and Charlier were captured, also Lieuts. Coffin, Powers and Curtice. Capt. Stone died in prison at Macon, Ga. Capts. Place and Charlier were exchanged eight months later, or in March, 1864. The three lieutenants were sent to Macon, and later to Charleston, S. C., where they were impounded with other officers under fire of the Union guns: but when six hundred rebel officers were sent down to Morris Island to be placed under fire, the Charleston commander removed the Yankee officers to a pen in rear of the city. And while Co. G had no representative among those officers, their hearts went out to them, and thus are they here remembered.

Eighty-six men were prisoners. Of those, thirty-seven accepted the parole offered by Gen. Lee and with about seventeen hundred others, were escorted to Gen. Couch's lines near Carlisle; the other forty-nine went to Richmond. There were ten of Co. G, prisoners, six of whom took the parole—two went to Richmond. The paroled prisoners were sent to Carlisle, Pa., where they were kept for awhile in fine style, and ultimately were returned to their regiments without exchange.

The company took into the fight about forty muskets.

KILLED.

Capt. Harrison Frank.
Albert D. Bridge.
John A. Hart.
Luzerne E. Johnson.
Durell Moore.

WOUNDED.

Lieut. Frank E. Gates, groin.
Corporal Jas. B. Hooper, arm.
Corporal Nicholas Binges, side.
Private Amos Avery, shoulder.
Private Peter Agan, leg.
Private Robert Farrington, arm.
Private Joseph Hart, leg.
Private Wm. Miller, hand.
Private Wm. Pease, leg.
Private James L. Travis, arm and shoulder.
Private John H. Roe, face.

Col. Brown was very much cast down over his losses. Who to blame, will never be known. There was a horrible blunder and some one was blamable. The 157th never should have been sent out against Dole's Brigade of Georgians.

They had fought two regiments alone and unaided. A wonder that any of the boys left that wheatfield unhurt.

That was only one of the many little blunders of the war. The North kept on bleeding and her officers never lacked words for defense. Nothing new and withal, consistent. The soldiers were there to give their lives, if need be, and a good soldier will not hesitate over so trifling a matter. There was glory in the air, though. One could fairly taste it when Lee turned back for Virginia with his heart heavy. The cause of secession and human slavery had started down to destruction and the people of the North rejoiced.

Yet there were many desolate homes in the North. The babes of the South and the babes of the North clung to their mothers' knees and asked them why they wept—mercifully were they denied a share in the glory of the hour. Aged parents sat in the corner and mourned, until they were reunited with their slaughtered boys. Ah, the fatalities in that war were not confined to the boys in blue.

The wounded men of the regiment were gathered together and cared for by surgeons of both armies, while the battle was pending. When the Union army gained possession of the village, everything possible was done to alleviate suffering. Nurses came from all directions; many women and among them Sisters of Charity. Theirs was a noble work.

Very feeble are words to express the tender care of the women nurses in the war. The youngster who pours over war history will drink in all the horrors of battle scenes, or feed his imagination with cannon smoke. He will not care to gather the groaning victims and bear them from the field. Then, the sickening odors of human blood which one scents everywhere. Yet, amid those dreadful scenes those nurses went. They bathed the fevered faces, they moistened the parching throats. From hastily appointed kitchens they supplied tempting broth, or by woman's magic produced cooling drinks.

The women of the war. History says little of them, but the hearts of thousands of soldiers are theirs.

July 5th the regiment was marched back toward Emmettsburg, eight miles. Next day the little band moved into that village. By calling in detatched men and by the return of all available men, the command had reached the number of eighty. Col. Brown was assigned to duty elsewhere. Maj. Carmichael was on the staff of Gen. Schurz. The command of the 157th devolved upon Capt. Bailey, with two or three lieutenants. They made two companies of the battalion and the state colors waved above them.

The honor of Lenox had been sorely tried at Gettysburg and the reduced ranks of Co's B and G bent now under the weight of responsibility. Still there was no shrinking, they were yet on a war-footing even if their shoes were dropping from their feet.

They were not a very attractive little band of warriors as they shuffled and limped into Middletown about 10 p. m., July 7th. But they were very thankful for a rain storm which softened the roads and thus eased the bruised feet. It had been a rough march over the Chitocton mountain, the sun pouring down hot, the pathway rough, with plenty of climbing. Thus they toiled over nearly twenty miles, encouraged on the way that shoes awaited them in Middletown; but they were disappointed.

A rest was given until the 9th and as the whereabouts of Lee was then known, the army was set in motion. On that day Co. G were on the road, their shoes were worn out and their feet very nearly so, but the boys made the best of it and dragged along in the hot, muggy atmosphere, over Smith Mountain, camping near Boonsboro after a very trying march of six miles only.

They lay at Boonsboro on the 10th, where shoes were issued. On the 11th the boys marched out on the Hagerstown Pike, in the advance and camped. Next day, July 12th, Major Carmichael assumed command. Col. Brown was temporarily at the head of a brigade in another division.

On the 10th Gen. Howard had issued his "General Order No. 18.—The General again thanks his command for what has been done during the last month..... The Eleventh Corps, as a Corps, has done well—well in marching, well in fighting. The sacrifices it has made shall not be forgotten—in the retrospect your General feels satisfied. Now we must make one more effort; let there be no wavering, no doubt."

That was a sickly sort of cheer to send to Co. G, the lonesome, the ragged and destitute. Yes, Gen. Howard, you are satisfied, but Co. G are not. They are forlorn. Their laurels hang over their brows, wilted and stale. You are not a vain man. But never forget, that a peacock may look "in the retrospect" and be satisfied. "Let there be no wavering, no doubt." Had that fine regiment but "wavered," General Howard, they would not now be so few.

Following is taken from Gen. Lee's "General Order No. 16," dated July 11th, 1863, to his defeated army: "Once more the eyes of your countrymen are turned upon you, and again do wives and sisters, fathers, mothers and helpless children lean for defense upon your strong arms and brave hearts." It was the production of an enemy, but just the sort of stuff to stir the blood of men. Lee knew if he showed lack of confidence in his men, he weakened them. But enough of this. The 11th Corps has fought hard and won a blackened eye on the pages of history. Occasionally they are "damned with faint praise," just to save the record of some general.

The 157th was at this time, July 12th, annexed to the first division of the 11th Corps, in the brigade commanded by Gen. Adelbert Ames.

On the morning of that day, with fresh accessions from hospitals and other sources, the 157th had increased its numbers to one hundred.

As they aproached Hagerstown they were deployed as skirmishers and advanced ahead of the cavalry. Two miles from Hagerstown the rebel rear-guard was encountered and a lively skirmish followed, but the 157th got the rebs started and kept them going until they were checked by a battery planted on the hights beyond the town.

As the battery opened the cavalry rushed forward and Co. G and their comrades came near losing their opportunities for distinction; soon however the cavalrymen came back in confusion.

Maj. Carmichael had screened his men from the hot, raking fire, by taking advantage of a broad ditch and as the cavalry returned, the boys started on a keen run for the town, which they reached successfully and under cover of the buildings were soon in possession of the city. With the enemy still in sight on the hights, their names were registered at the Washington Hotel, directly following those of the rebel officers who had stopped there the night before.

Fifty prisoners were captured in different parts of the town and among them, two wounded officers, from the field of Gettysburg.

As a mark of distinction the 157th were distributed over the town on provost duty. Hagerstown had five or six thousand inhabitants. This duty continued for two days; meanwhile they can be credited to date.

The 157th had turned over to the provost marshal of the Army, one hundred prisoners. At Gettysburg they had lost but eighty-six of their men prisoners, besides seven officers. As one officer ought to count for two men, the regiment has vindicated itself, with a heavy credit balance in its favor of more than two hundred and sixty causalties. As to prisoners, they have seldom found glory in being captured. They attract much sympathy, but there is usually an ugly "if" lurking in the background. The dead are heroes. 'Tis well.

July 14th Col. Brown returned to his regiment and the major to duty as mustering officer on Schurz's staff.

On that afternoon Co. G were marched out to within two miles of Williamsport, in search of Gen. Lee. The regiment camped in a pine wood. Next day, the 15th, they were countermarched twenty miles to Middletown over the road they had come. Lee's army had escaped, and Co. G, like the loyal people of the North, were hunting for some secluded place where they could quietly kick themselves, undisturbed, and get cool.

The 16th found them en route to Berlin, camping within two miles of that place, after a tramp of twelve miles. They lay there until the 19th and then marched to the Potomac and crossed on the pontoon bridge, camping three miles beyond Waterford. They took an early start on the 20th and marched to Groveton, Va. While there they were sent on a wild-goose chase after Moseby's cavalry, who were supposed to be in the vicinity of Mt. Pleasant. On the 23d of July they moved to Middleburg—a secesh town where all the ladies kept behind the blinds—camping at night at White Plains. On the 24th the boys reached New Baltimore. July 25th the regiment marched to Warrenton Junction having found at last, the close of the campaign.

The boys were not very attractive in appearance when they left Gettysburg and they had not improved greatly by an additional twenty days' march. They were short of soap and of underwear. In many cases where neglect seemed inviting him, a well-known pest appeared, and skirmishing, "with vigor and alacrity," was not considered unbecoming to many a dignified officer. Truth is stranger than fiction, and here effect follows cause in close pursuit. At last however time was allowed for cleaning up, and those boys were not slow to make the most of such glad hours. The subject is not pleasant.

As has been intimated, the troops around Warrenton were not entirely idle. Considerable picket-duty was required. On the 1st of August they moved to Greenwich, so named after one Green, who claimed British protection, and the flag of Britain waved above his spacious mansion.

On the 3d camp was moved to near Catlett Station. At midnight of the 6th orders came to be ready to take the cars on short notice. Next day, the 7th, the little squad of Co. G heard the order to go into camp. They had done so much tramping that a prospect of a free ride, for a time seemed dissipated. They grumbled not— the grumblers had been captured and were eating pie and pudding at Carlisle. At noon the skies brightened and the bold Co. G were to shake the soil of Virginia from their feet for all time.

Gordon's division, which included Ames' brigade, moved to Warrenton Junction and the same night took comfortable freight cars for Alexandria. On the car tops were the able-bodied men and on the first floor were the sick and the officers, with scarcely room to stretch themselves. The train reached Alexandria at 5 a. m. The men alighted and partook of a soldier's breakfast in a field near the depot. At noon they were taken to a steamer and next day were at Newport News.

Newport News had been a favored camping place, from the first of the war. When Co. G. with skin as tender as their hearts, stepped ashore, multitudes of hungry fleas, gnats and mosquitos attacked them and the poor boys were once more suffering for the cause of freedom.

Ten days' rations were issued before leaving Catlett. The officers now discovered that the men were in a way to hunger before the journey was ended. For it is true of men everywhere— some are prodigal by nature.

On the evening of the 9th of August Co. G found themselves aboard a steamship and bounding on the billows of the Atlantic. They sailed under sealed orders. In all games of chance strategy is recognized. Secretary Stanton was about to send a few thousands of troops to re-enforce Gen. Gilmore.

Co. G was not entirely happy. Besides a slight sympathy with the rolling ocean, they were wondering just how bad they would be missed by their critics in the 1st Army Corps. Alas, little did they know of the future—how high and in what black letters would the fame of the 11th Corps be written by jealous pens.

And thoughts, longing, sweet and bitter, burdened the hour. Finally they went into the scuppers, and as Cape Henry dropped into the deep, they washed from their noble forms the last accumulation of Virginia soil. The parting was not pathetic.

Rightly named and suitable for the operations before Charleston, was the new camping place of Gordon's division. There was as high standard of tom-foolery in that department as in any, during the war. And for some time Folly Island served as a base.

Stono Inlet was reached on the 12th of August. The trip was made without incident. Co. G had gathered along the rail of the John Rice and they bit huge chunks from the sea breeze; for it was "hotter than—here—Hamilton!" below decks, as John Miller would have said, had he been present.

In the evening of the 12th Co. G stepped to the floating wharf (an old hulk) at Pawnee landing and for the first time pressed the sacred soil of South Carolina. They had tried hard to reach the seat of rebellion at Richmond and failed. They had now come to the original incubator for another attempt. Charleston was still defiant and Co. G were on Folly Island.

Oh, brave Co. G, you were born heroes. Why did Fate thus trifle with your yearnings for fame?

The day following the landing, the 157th moved two miles up the island, or half way between Stono and Light House Inlet.

On the 16th they were marched up the beach to the rope ferry and crossed to Morris Island, and proceeded to duty in the advance parallels of the approaches.

Gen. Gilmore was trying to reduce Fort Wagner. One month before, a desperate battle was fought, with great loss to the Union forces. Then Gilmore began his siege. The troops worked hard and were sure of unearthing the enemy if the sand of Morris Island held out.

Duty in the bomb-proofs was very trying. The heat was oppressive and fresh air very scarce. With other discomforts, sand fleas were very plentiful. Whenever the rebel fire slackened, the boys got out and exercised. Three days of such miserable experience were quite enough for them, but they were detailed again and again. Perhaps it was during that siege Co. G replenished their stock of sand, as the boys insisted they breathed it and ate sand with their food, and it blew into their mouths when they were talking, and into their eyes, and into their ears.

On the 21st of August Gen. Terry reviewed the troops in Gordon's division. Those men had not been supplied with new clothing since the Gettysburg campaign and Terry was disposed to censure their shabby appearance. For his brigade, Gen. Ames made a proper explanation and concluded with something after this style—

"But, General, if you have any fighting for us,

you will see that we understand our duty and will obey orders."

August 27th the division returned to Folly Island and went into camp four miles from Light House Inlet.

Sept. 6th Ames' brigade, consisting of six regiments numbering less than five hundred men, were taken to the front on Morris Island as a portion of an assaulting column to advance next morning at 9 o'clock. During the night a deserter came into Gilmore's lines and reported the rebels evacuating the fort. Fort Wagner had at last come into Yankee hands, and was re-christened Fort Strong, in memory of Gen. Strong, who led the assault on the fort, July 11th. He was dangerously wounded, and died at New York, a few weeks later.

Up to this period the regiment was composed of two companies. Men were returning from hospitals and parole camp. The ranks of Co. G were steadily increasing in numbers as also were the other companies. Their duties were not severe, but the change of water affected some of the boys badly.

With the exception of a night alarm, when the long-roll was beaten, there was very little to vary the monotony of life among the sand hills. To be sure the regiment was camped in a grove of small live-oaks, but behind the camp was a sand ridge and sand, dry sand, was the prevailing soil.

Bathing was a necessity, and at a prescribed hour the beach for miles was patronized by the men.

Col. Brown had left the regiment at New Baltimore, Va., for recruiting service at Elmira, N. Y. Major Carmichael was now lieutenant colonel and commanded the 157th.

For some weeks Col. Carmichael was confined to his tent. Then the camp was a dull place. Eventually the days became brighter. New clothing was issued, the wormy hard-bread gave way to good soft loaves, and soldiering was soldiering once more.

Captain Lafayette McWilliams was not a "boy of Lenox." He enlisted in Co. F, at Peterboro and was made third sergeant of his company. At Chancellorsville he acted as adjutant of the regiment, was taken prisoner and was sent to Libby prison. Rejoined the regiment just before the Gettysburg fight and was assigned temporarily to the quartermaster's department. He was left in Virginia when the regiment went South, and returned to duty early in September, duly commissioned as captain of Co. G. His first essay at speech-making was in censure of the boys captured at Gettysburg. His remarks, for one who was not in the fight, were very extraordinary. Co. G, in that fight did well. One of the boys was captured supporting his dying captain. Two others assisted a badly wounded and fainting man (of another company) to the regimental hospital; and not knowing the proximity of the rebels, ran into their clutches, very much as did Adjutant McWilliams at Chancellorsville. Col. Brown went through the streets with one man of Co. G, who bore the colors. All organization was destroyed. Who was blamable? Was there anything praiseworthy in the acts of the men of Co. G on that dreadful day?

Long did some of the boys hold spite against their new captain for his unkind words, until they understood that he had been wrongly informed. And when they became better known to each other, unpleasant differences vanished.

Lafayette McWilliams was an excellent officer. He took pride in the good appearance of his men. Co. G, under their new captain, throve finely. The honor of old Lenox was again a light burden.

Carmichael's ideal soldier was a possibility. Brown's ideal was a mixture of puritanic devotion and Napoleonic dash.

"Keep the men clean; nourish manly pride; make them feel that they are men; treat them in a way to gain their confidence, and you will have soldiers you can depend upon. Drill him as you may, a man without pride is unreliable;" such was the doctrine of Col. Carmichael.

Camp was moved further up the river and A tents were issued. From a convenient pine grove the boys cut posts and sunk them into the sand. Then they raised the tents upon the posts and had roomy space, with plenty of standing room. The bunks were built well above ground and the lower part around the tents enclosed with the old shelter tents.

It was an attractive camp on the white sand, and the boys were in better health. An eating house was built of pine poles and roofed with palmetto leaves. Tables and seats were erected and the men were marched in regularly to their meals.

For spiritual food the chaplain served his preparations on Sundays, when Gen. Ames occasionally dropped over to attend.

There were regular duties on picket at the White House, with an occasional detail to Coles Island, or Kiawah. The details to Kaiwah were for fatigue duty on fortifications and they were pleasant, owing to freedom from the strict discipline of camp. Mud clams were abundant in the creeks over there.

Picket duty at the White House on Folly River, was attractive as the cold weather approached, on account of the abundance of cluster oysters which lined the banks. Those oysters, when taken from the shells, were usually very small—from the size of one's finger nail, to an inch in length.

Dan Brockway saw his opportunity. It was a happy day for him when he was detailed for picket at the White House. When off post he was picking open the shells, and far into the night while others slept, Dan was still at work, until he had secured a good quart, which he sold to officers for about fifty cents; and well he earned his money. Often the orderly's voice was heard in the camp calling. "Brockway!" Brock was either out after oysters or with haversacks loaded with apples, was peddling in other camps.

That sort of thing must end. The captain declared it should end. One day Brock was arraigned in presence of Co. G, and the punishment he merited seemed imminent.

"Captain," says Brock, "I have only a halfbarrel of apples left, and they will spoil if you don't let me sell them."

"Very well," replied the captain. "But you must promise, hereafter to attend to duty."

Brock promised and escaped punishment, but that half-barrel of apples lasted a long time. It appeared he had another supply by means of which he kept the first barrel from being exhausted.

At Folly Island, for the first time, men were detailed in each company to wash the clothing of the men and all were of a uniform cleanliness, and the wash-squad did their work well.

The regimental organization was again complete. In November a detachment of substitutes and drafted men reached the regiment; of those Co. G received five men.

And there came also from Elmira a new adjutant for the 157th. Chas. J. Baldwin was an inexperienced soldier. He had been acting as Col. Brown's adjutant at Elmira and was promoted on personal grounds. There was an unconfirmed report that he was a drafted man. Had he been so, or had Baldwin been a veteran of many battles, Col. Brown's thus slighting his regiment, would have been no less unfair. Baldwin was a good man, made a fine adjutant. Perhaps he was innocent of an intent to appropriate the position which was clearly due one of those men who had seen so much hard service.

Col. Brown detailed Joseph Heenye to be his personal waiter. Then he promoted him to sergeant-major of the regiment. While Joe Heenye was enjoying the comforts and privileges of exemption from drill, from camp duty and from picket, the other enlisted men were out in the sleet and the snow and the mud. While Joe slept in a warm bed every night, his comrades slept out in the dismal picket huts. No fault of Joe's. But when he was promoted adjutant over the heads of many worthy lieutenants, Col. Brown added greatly to the offense. Joe was a gentleman. He was killed at Gettysburg.

Col. Brown from a settled policy, promoted officers and assigned them to other companies than those in which they had enlisted. Such a scheme was an exhibition of his arbitrary power and in some instances the effect was demoralizing. When Lieut. Gates was transferred to Co. K, the boys of his own company wondered and Co. K were offended. By and by, Lieut. Pierce was assigned from Co. K to Co. G, and the scale was righted. And when Bob Grant was made first lieutenant of Co. G, his own company, Co. I, were inconsolable and the philosophical Co. G, were correspondingly pleased.

That system of crossing-the-breed was peculiar to Col. Brown. Had the good people of Madison discovered such propensity in time, undoubtedly they would have suggested that Prof. Brown seek a colonelcy in some other county. But the regiment is still on Folly Island.

Such a pity so good a regiment should have seen so much trifling. And even yet were they to steam up rivers, to march, to camp, to wade swamps, to fight and hang-on, for many months to come and after it all, not one enterprise in which they were engaged—barring the siege of Charleston—in that Department, has been deemed worthy of place in standard history. The stubs of Gen. Grant's cigars, the white vests of Gen. Sherman and the peculiar cast of Gen. Butler's eye, all are immortal. Poor Co. G, you are making history and your valiant deeds shall be chronicled. And your children may know, that while brave and true men were required to perform these deeds, even the weakest of men may record them. Such is fate.

In the latter part of December, Col. Carmichael was ordered North with a recruiting party; winter had reached South Carolina, and in the morning thin ice frequently was found upon the surface of bathing tubs. Not the pleasantest season to journey northward.

As the weather grew colder drinking water was more agreeable. All the water used on the island was obtained by digging below tide-mark and curbing with barrels. The finest and best protected well in camp was made by cutting into a sand dune and making a winding passage to the water, thus placing the water continually in the shade and protecting it from dust and dirt blowing around the camp.

The regiment remained on Folly Island until February 7th, 1864, when orders came to prepare for a march with three days' rations and forty rounds of ammunition. At dusk they were ferried over to Kiawah Island. Three brigades and two batteries formed the expedition. They marched up Kiawah, forded the narrow creek to Seabrook, and then over the bridge to John's Island, tramping until daybreak, when they found themselves near the center of the island. A line of skirmishers under Lieut. Gates was thrown forward to meet the advancing rebels, then a lively exchange of shots ensued, resulting in the enemy falling back. Next the brigade was advanced about a mile until they came up with the skirmishers. A large quantity of arms and accoutrements were found in some buildings near Edisto River and were destroyed. The rebels were found well posted behind a hedge. The first brigade fell back again and bivouaced. Next day the second brigade went to the front and stirred up the rebs a little. The third day the first brigade (in which was Co. G) again went to the front and supported a battery. At midnight the pickets were withdrawn and after setting fire to a mansion the expedition returned to Folly Island. The demonstration was to draw the enemy from the army opposing Gen. Seymour, who was then about to fight the disastrous battle of Olustee, Florida.

In that trip to John's Island one man was killed and one wounded, of the 157th regiment, both of Co. I.

On the 22nd of February Co. G, under Lieut. Grant, (Capt. McWilliams had gone north with Col. Carmichael) were ordered to pack up, for Gen. Seymour had been roughly handled and he wanted Co. G to come down to Jacksonville with the other boys. Gen. Seymour had exceeded his instructions. He deserved to have been cashiered, but Grant ordered him North, gave him another command, and the rebs soon after captured him.

The 157th landed in Jacksonville Feb. 25th, 1864, with two hundred and eighty-six muskets, or one hundred less than at Gettysburg. They were commanded by Col. Brown.

The trip down was very unpleasant for the men on the lower deck and a number of them were sea-sick. The comments of Nick Snyder and John Miller can be left to the imagination of readers. For they felt glad they were fighting for Yankee land, instead of beastly, blasted, blinkety-blank ships on a r-r-rolling ocean.

Feb. 25th the boys landed at Jacksonville, at the time only a good sized village. Gen. Ames led his men to the outskirts. Rumors came of a threatened attack and preparations were made accordingly. It may be put down, here at once, that no rebel ever attacked Jacksonville (except by rumor) during Co. G's stay at the place, and if any other of the companies had been attacked, Co. G would have heard of it, promptly.

In a day or two the regiment was busy with picks and shovels, throwing up breast-works and redoubts, nor did the work stop until a line was built nearly a mile in length. The redoubts were protected with chevre du frieze and trip-wires were stretched along the front of the works.

The regiment had been eating hard-tack for some time because facilities for supplying them with fresh loaves were not perfected. Capt. Gates obtained leave to draw flour from the commissary and arrange a bakery for his company. He took possession of a bakery in town, detailed men, with Ike Perry of Co. H at their head, and in a short time Co. K were eating fresh bread. The plan succeeded so well that the bakery was called upon to supply the regiment.

The bakery was a saving scheme, for the flour allowed by the government, was in excess of the amount required for an abundant supply of bread, and in a few weeks hundreds of dollars commutation for such excess was allowed the 157th.

At Folly Island Col. Carmichael had organized a brass band and armed those men with a varied assortment of instruments. The grand revelation at Jacksonville in the one item of bread, opened a way to purchasing a set of fine German silver instruments. Strange it was that Capt. Gates was soon after relieved from the bread management and from that time, the regimental fund ceased to be a matter of history. The query often passed around the camp—if two hundred men can save a thousand dollars in a few weeks by commutation of rations, how much should a regiment or an army save in one year? and from one item of bread. The good people at home, also were being bled by army sharks.

This little work is not designed for the purpose of paying-off old grudges. The above item is history. Col. Brown, let it be known, is believed to have been innocent of any meanness in providing for his men. They usually were well supplied with plenty of good food. He looked after their sanitary welfare, and in proof of this last assertion can be given the fact that during its entire service, no severe epidemic raged among the men. Credit is due also to the surgeons of the regiment, Drs. Hendrick, Crawe and Beebe, who were faithful in the performance of their duties.

During the battle of Gettysburg Dr. Crawe remained in the town; and while shells were flying over and bullets pattering against the walls, faithfully, with other Union surgeons, continued to labor for the relief of the suffering wounded.

While work was being done on the fortifications regular details were sent out for picketing. And with all preparations for a reception the rebels did not come.

Pollard in his "Lost Cause," says, the battle of Olustee "was decisive, as it resulted in the expulsion of the enemy from Florida, and the preservation of this state to the Confederacy." Co. G did not agree with Mr. Pollard of Richmond, any more than they agreed with those Army of the Potomac critics who so strongly intimate that when Jackson drove back the 11th Corps at Chancellorsville the Army of the Potomac was defeated. The 11th Corps never assumed to be the bulwark of that army. Gen. Seymour was not the forlorn hope of the North. The brigade of Gen. Ames was soon to hold Jacksonville, St. Augustine and Fernandina. Co. G was not so easily expelled.

On the 12th of April came the news that the brigade was to be dissolved and Gen. Ames was ordered north with the 10th Corps. Co G had never seen that army corps assembled during the six months they had been attached. While on the John's Island excursion they were in the largest assemblage of that corps with whom they ever had marched. There "Little Shimmel" was at their head once more, in charge of the expedition, and the general had not forgotten them. The boys had learned to like Gen. Ames, because he was a good officer, if a little rough at times. This new arrangement made the 144th and the 157th N. Y. regiments virtually the town guard at Jacksonville. The 17th Conn. was sent to St. Augustine and the 107th Ohio to Fernandina, while the 75th Ohio was to be mounted for scouting purposes. To these forces should be added the artillery and not least, the gunboats in the river.

In the month of March one hundred recruits arrived who had been secured by the recruiting party under Col. Carmichael; they were soon after followed by that officer and his attachment. Of those recruits Co. G received twenty-two, increasing the company to about forty men. With but few exceptions those new men were excellent material.

To those boys of Lenox it seemed always summer, a country where snow never fell; yet, they knew spring had come in Florida, when the magnolias spread their blossoms.

The trying experiences of Jacksonville were at an end. No more digging by day and by night, no more sleeping in those trenches to be preyed upon by fleas. The regiment was to be divided.

One hot morning, April 21st, 1864, the boys moved down to the St. John's river. Companies A, B, C, D, E and F under Col. Brown, embarked upon one boat for Fernandina, and Co. G, H, I and K under Col. Carmichael, on another boat, for Picolata twenty-five miles up the river.

With Col. Brown went the state colors and the band. With the Picolata detachment was the beautiful flag presented the regiment by the ladies of Cortland.

When the two boats swung out into the stream the boys cheered, and moisture gathered in some eyes, for it was the parting of a family. Then the band struck up a lively tune, and a bend in the river intervened, drawing the attention of Co. G to the subject of torpedoes. The gunboats and other boats, most of them, were provided each with a torpedo-rake at the bows, nevertheless there was great uncertainty in the air as well as in the dark colored water upon which they were riding. At the wide water some distance above Jacksonville, lay two large sidewheel steamers, sunk by torpedoes. On one of these boats a large number of colored troops perished. The trip was not entirely comfortable and Co. G was too intently listening, to note many really novel and entertaining features of this first excursion on the upper waters. There was danger,as afterwards proved, as a steamer was sunk near Jacksonville shortly after. So when Picolata was reached the boys were not sorry to step on dry land.

The 157th boys relieved a detachment of colored troops, pitched their tents under the trees and softened their beds with gray moss.

Duty at Picolata was picketing. Men were sent up the river to Orange Mills and to other points. At night a picket boat lay in the river below the post. Really, the Picolata station was an outpost of St. Augustine some twelve or fourteen miles distant. It was a crossing point on the St. John's.

The river is sluggish and water coming from many swamps is not wholesome. For a few days the men drank river water, then barrels were filled and brought into camp from springs outside the lines and drinking from the river was prohibited. Dr. Crawe, to whom the matter was referred, decided the water of the St. John's was well-fitted for breeding alligators, but not wholesome as a beverage for men.

As an additional safeguard, a small stockade was erected in the rear of the camp, armed with two small brass pieces which had been captured at Pilatka, a few months previous. To man those guns men were detailed from the post and drilled by an artilleryman.

On the 27th of April, Gen. Birney came up the river with a colored regiment and two steamers. Companies G, H, and K were ordered to draw fourteen days' rations and to be supplied with sixty rounds of cartridges, all of which was promptly done and the colonel and his three companies embarked on the small steamer, Harriet Weed. Then, convoyed by the gunboat Ottawa the expedition moved up the river. The gunboat stopped opposite Pilatka—not an inhabitant was in sight—and the huge amidships gun bore threatening upon the small city. Leaving the Ottawa, the other steamers passed up the River to Welaka, where Co. G was hurried ashore and thrown out as skirmishers, while the other troops were rapidly landing and getting into line. With a guide, the 157th in the advance, the column proceeded up the river. It was a dark night, the deep foliage along the roadside added to the gloom.

Soon after dark the boys reached a house. For some reason Col. Carmichael suspected a rebel was hidden about the premises. A search was made and he was found hiding under the house. When the man was brought forth, his family made pitiful appeals, to which the colonel kindly replied, assuring them the union troops would take good care of Mr. Shook, who was blacksmith for the troop called Steven's cavalry. And so the unfortunate man was marched away from his weeping family, a prisoner of war.

Gen. Birney halted the column near old Fort Gates (a relic of the Seminole war) and the boys laid down behind their stacked arms. They had been asleep but a little while when a gun was fired, then another, and more.

Col. Carmichael called his men to "attention" and they stood at their guns, until it was learned that the colored pickets had mistaken shadows for men moving about. Co. G were again nicely dreaming the hours away, when bang! bang! went the guns.

"Lie still, boys," said the colonel, "there is nothing out there but stumps and bushes."

And the tired men snuggled down under their blankets, not very well pleased with the picket-line.

Next day, the 28th, the column left the river and marched out into the country, halting at a place called Granville Priests, a small and varied assortment of poor houses and negro cabins. At that place the 157th parted from Gen. Birney and the colored regiment.

At Priests a fine lot of sweet potatoes were found. The cooks arranged their kettles and the boys held a feast.

Col. Carmichael and his men were ordered to return to Picolata driving as many cattle as could be secured. Native herdsmen were employed and the colonel, with no escort, started with them, all mounted, in advance of his men, promising to await them at Middle Haw Creek.

Capt. McWilliams was then ranking officer. He led his men to Middle Haw and camped. The colonel was not there and every one worried, for they knew he was among natives.

Next day, April 30th, they were marched fourteen miles through the pine woods and saw no house until reaching Sander's corral. There they found a sort of cabin built of poles, raised two feet above the ground. There, also, they found Col. Carmichael, safe and sound, with several herdsmen and a large drove of cattle, and when night dropped over the scene the epicures of the detachment gathered a few of the Sanders chickens.

The door of the cabin suddenly opened and a tall woman appeared, holding high a lighted candle.

"Colonel," she screamed, "your men are taking my chickens. I heard them squawking."

"Oh, no, madam, I guess they will not hurt your chickens?" was the reply.

It was fine to have the colonel a little hard of hearing, sometimes. Very well he knew his boys had no hold on any chicken that "squawked." Some chicken roosts were too near the house, anyway.

May 1st was Sunday. The route led over the usual flat country, through stretches of pine, across savannas, and occasionally here and there a basin-shaped pond or sink-hole. The column passed around the head of Dunn's Lake, the boys supplying themselves with sour oranges from trees near the landing. At night they bivouaced near a corral. They had made eighteen miles.

The boys of Co. G long remembered the camp of that night near Dunn's Lake. It was decided that one of the herd should be butchered. John Wise of Co. G was the butcher of the detachment, but the night in question he politely waived his privilege and an officer was allowed to do the shooting. The result was amazing. The poor creature had been driven all day and yet was strong enough, when dressed, to have pulled a cart. He was a patriarch of the herd. And the boys cut him into small bits and toasted him on sharpened sticks; they threw the meat on the coals to see it curl up like bark; they nibbled at it, they tried to chew it, but the patriarch was to be eaten only in lumps. Many compliments were launched at John Wise, who came forward, explained and was excused. For John was a good fellow.

May 2d was the anniversary of the Chancellorsville fight. After an easy march camp was reached about 5 p. m., at Middleton's farm. As evening came on the cows were driven into a yard and milked by women. No milking stools were necessary, as the native cow of Florida is built on the elevated plan. Milkers placed their heads in front of the cow's hip and slightly bending, drew the milk into the gourd. Each cow yielded nearly one quart of milk, or as one woman said, the forty cows gave, "I reckon, about a bushel." Co. G gathered around the corrall and when milking was over they held out their canteens and had them filled, paying for the milk in cash. When Colonel Carmichael said, "no foraging," he was obeyed.

May 3d the boys marched to Moccasin Branch, an easy tramp of eight miles. There they found the most primitive methods of farm life in the wilderness, still in operation. The old man had his tan vat behind the house. A stump was scooped out to serve as a mortar for making samp or hominy. His apparatus for sugar-making—the rollers for crushing cane and the sugar out-fit generally, all were of the simplest design. But the sour oranges there were fully up-to-date in their intensity.

May 4th, after an absence of one week, Co. G found themselves again in camp at Picolata. The detachment had marched one hundred miles and brought in fifteen hundred cattle of all sizes and ages. Co. G were becoming accustomed to good old Florida beef. The cattle were taken to Jacksonville for army and navy consumption.

The jaunt was rather enjoyed by the old trampers. On the recruits, however, it bore heavily, that being their first march in harness; but they did remarkably well.

The routine of camp life was again established, and quite easy it was. The heat of a far southern sun was becoming stronger and the boys felt languid. Moored along the river banks were dozens of dug-outs of every pattern, prizes taken along the shores; and these little boats afforded a diversion for any who could handle them. Some of the boys set night-lines and caught cat-fish. Others fished at night with torch and spear for the gar fish. Alligators were often seen floating with the current, or at night they were heard among the rushes bellowing like young bulls. Occasionally an alligator was shot.

The greatest pests Co. G found in Florida were mosquitoes and gnats. Many a blacksnake was seen with an occasional venomous snake, and water snakes, but no member of the regiment was bitten although they spread their blankets for the night, on the ground, without thought or precaution. Often small scorpions were found in the tents and rarely a centipede. But fleas were sometimes secreted in the hanging moss.

East Florida in those days, was mostly wilderness. Deer and other game abounded. Outside the picket line, for some time, the men on post were frequently annoyed by prowling wildcats, whose running about and snarling, broke the monotony of dark nights.

The view about Picolata was very pleasant when the plains were bright with flowers, when the land appeared worthy of its fair name. Florida is much improved in population and thrift in these later days and may be enjoyable. But for all their sunshine and flowers, their oranges and " 'arly sarce," Co. G would not, in 1864, have parted with a single square acre out of old Lenox,—not for all East Florida.

Sunday, May 22nd, while the Picolata force were drawn up for inspection, two steamers arrived, together with the gunboat Ottawa.

Before this time, Col. Brown had been ordered to Hilton Head as Provost Marshall of the Department of the South. That change made Col. Carmichael ranking officer and he accordingly made requisition for companies A and F and also for the band, all of whom were at Fernandina.

Maj. Place had returned from imprisonment, and came up to Picolata in charge of the two companies. When the boys marched aboard the gunboat Ottawa the major was left in charge of the camp.

This time a landing was made opposite Pilatka, the men halting for the night seven miles further up the river.

May 23d the column marched to Middle Haw Creek, nearly twenty miles, reaching camp at 9 p. m. A junction was made there with troops from St. Augustine.

May 24th was hot and sultry. One day's rations were issued and the boys took the back-track for Picolata.

Near noon a halt was made near a large water hole and the men were told to fill their canteens, as no more water would be found until night. In the afternoon as they moved along the narrow trail they grew very thirsty, so that long before night many of the canteens were empty. As the night came on and no water was found, Col Carmichael suspected some trickery from the guide, and he detailed two men with loaded pieces to escort the man and to shoot upon the first indication of treachery. And so they moved along, the poor guide insisting that he was right, only he had miscalculated distance. The boys of the 144th N. Y., were suffering from thirst and their colonel ordered his pioneers to dig for water. The guide called out,

"You'll not get water there."

"Where will we find it?" growled back a chorus of voices.

"Jist about two mile from yere."

"Are you sure?" asked Col. Carmichael.

"Yes, cunnel, I'm dead sure."

The colonel called to several mounted officers and away they all went out into the darkness. Co. G sank upon the ground and waited patiently. After a time the colonel returned and reported water a short distance ahead and marching about a mile they reached Middleton's and were again on familiar ground. It was midnight before the boys had drank their coffee and were under the blankets. They were very tired, having marched thirty miles.

March 25, an easy march was promised the men and they made eight miles to Moccasin Branch, where they halted for dinner. Again taking the road the march was increased to thirteen miles, part of the way through a brisk summer shower.

The boys were halted that night in a lane not far from the shack where the colonel was quartered. Air to breathe seemed scarce and fleas appeared to be unusually active. At the miserable house the officers, lying on the floor, were much annoyed by the persistent occupation of hogs underneath them. Fleas gnawed the officers and they scratched and scolded. Fleas tortured the saw-backs and they humped themselves and rubbed against the floor-joists, and as they toiled they grunted. Out in the lane the men of Co. G were too busy to sleep. That little farm in the wilderness might have been the main supply station for all East Florida fleadom.

It was an easy march May 26th of only nine miles to Picolata. When the boys approached the camp Maj. Place came out to meet them with the band. Then Co. G braced up in style and stepped off to the good old tune of "The Girls We Left Behind Us." Co. G remembered the girls.

The object of the expedition, besides giving the boys an outing, was to gather up any loose rebels in the vicinity of Dunn's Lake. Probably there were more soldiers in that command alone than the rebels had in the entire state of Florida at the time. There was no accounting for novelties in the department, illustrative of experimental or theoretical campaigning. And while Folly Island was anchored permanently, its suggestive and appropriate title was indelibly stamped upon nearly every expedition organized in the Department, from September, 1863, until the close of the war.

It was an extensive experiment station for the engineer officers of the army and for the navy. There they could study the flight of missles and their force; the relative difference in guns and mortars, and resistance of sand and iron armor. In short, it was a safe school where many a favorite matriculated and from which very few graduated. It was called warfare, because there were hospitals there and many graves.

Soon after the return from the second excursion, Col. Carmichael with fifty picked men were taken across the river and landed near Green Cove Springs. They proceeded into the country, returning next day, having captured a rebel mail and several horses.

On Sunday, May 29th, two regiments came over from St. Augustine and the 157th boys were ordered to be ready to move at noon with four day's rations and sixty rounds of cartridges and rubber blanket or piece of shelter tent. The men were drawn up in line, expecting to move, and were finally returned to their quarters.

Next day a boat came up from below and Co. G, as night fell over the tropical scene, stepped once again upon a steamer and near midnight found themselves behind the works in front of Jacksonville.

The morning of the 31st the sun rose angry. Co. G still lay behind the works. There was mystery all around them; a sort of mystery peculiar to the climate—a lazy mystery. Co. G did not broach the mystery—when they were wanted, was time enough for them.

As soon as darkness came, the boys were marched aboard of a steamer and were taken about eighteen miles up the river and landed at the mouth of a creek, on the west bank.

It was long past bedtime when the boys laid themselves down to rest—3 o'clock in the morning. They were allowed to sleep until near daybreak and were then aroused very quietly, lest the rebels should hear. No fires were allowed and any boy who lighted a pipe, did so very slyly. The men were told to eat something, then to fill their canteens from a neighboring brook, as no more water would be found before night—a delightful country, that land of flowers.

Col. Noble of the 17th Conn., (a dignified officer whose hair was very gray) commanded the party. All officers were dismounted.

Soon after daylight the column started. It was composed of three or four regiments, one of them colored.

As the day lengthened, the heat grew intense. At noon time it was so hot the birds ceased their callings, butterflies took to cover; the horny leaves of the palmetto scrub curled as the corn leaves curl and twist under an August sun. Not the slightest breeze stirred the air; there was a bluish haze in the atmosphere.

As often it occurs on such a march, some of the men drink all the water in their canteens before the day is half gone. With care three pints of water can be made to last a long time. And on the present occasion, long before night, many of the men carried empty canteens. Among the colored men the suffering was marked. They became desperate and threatened to leave the column. Col. Noble finally drew a revolver and ordered them into the ranks.

At nightfall Camp Milton was reached, preparations were made for a battle. Co. G were thrown forward as skirmishers and advanced. The rebels had retreated.

Plenty of water was found in a narrow stream

and the boys enjoyed their first cup of coffee of that day. They had marched thirty-two miles.

While they were eating their breakfast next morning, the pickets were driven in. As soon as possible Co. G were thrown forward. Pickets in front of them were firing rapidly. Co. G with arms at trail moved out in front a quarter of a mile, but saw nothing to shoot. The boys were not surprised—they had once camped on Folly Island.

Near noon the expedition started for Jacksonville, the 157th as rear guard. All went well until Camp Finnegan, twelve or fifteen miles from Jacksonville was reached. (Camps Milton and Finnegan were rebel camps). While crossing a small creek the enemy appeared on the opposite side of the clearing and opened fire at long range. A colored company, thrown out to cover the crossing, replied to the rebels. Again was Co. G ordered into skirmish line and their Enfield rifles soon closed the battle. One or two men were slightly wounded.

Many of the boys suffered on this return march, even more than on the preceding day. But they reached Jacksonville without further incident and were taken at once to the river and aboard a steamer. The events of the day had excited the people at headquarters and Col. Carmichael was ordered to again land his men and march them to the trenches for the night. He appealed for rations and was referred to the Sanitary Commission Agent, who issued to the 157th a barrel of milk crackers. The boys made the most of their opportunities, and soon were asleep in their old trenches at Jacksonville, and for the last time.

Next day, June 3d, the regiment went aboard a steamer and returned to Picolata.

The touring experience of Co. G in Florida was not luxurious. And when, after about four months stay, orders came to pack up and leave Picolata, not a regret was heard.

June 12th they swung away from the dock and the same evening were at Fernandina, and where amidst a chorus of "hellos!" the regiment was once more united.

On the 13th, the detachment in which was Co. G started for Hilton Head. The wind was right ahead and the vessel, a ferryboat; she pounded the sea like a thresher, and the captain put back to Fernandina. There they lay until the 16th of June, when the sea went down and the voyage was completed.

Co. G landed at Hilton Head on Thursday and went into camp. On the Saturday following a deserter belonging to another regiment was shot and Co. G was compelled to witness the execution. Poor deserter. Alas, for Co. G, to be drawn up to witness the killing of a man in cold blood! There were some phases of military life more brutal even than battles. Some formalities in the infliction of penalties, more horrible than the crime itself. And it is doubtful if the lesson thus taught, is made more impressive by a display of cruel ceremony. And the cowardice of the custom. No good soldier need be thus reminded that desertions in the face of the enemy is death. Let us hope, as time goes on, the nation will demand that unnecessary torture be avoided in warfare—that in order to punish one man, it is not necessary to torture his comrades.

Camp at Hilton Head was located out on the barren sand. During the day the tents were intolerably hot and for guards about the camp screens were built to shield them from the sun. At night cool breezes came in from the ocean and then the boys forgot the hungry fleas and slumbered.

Rigid sanitary rules were enforced. Ice was

obtained from the Sanitary Commission to cool the lips of the sick ones in the hospital tent, and a barrel was kept supplied with iced water for general drinking purposes. That barrel, the boys will remember, was for some reason noticeably charged with the flavor of Tommy Reagan's "nice swate vinegar."

There was considerable sickness among the men and several deaths in the regiment.

The discharge of the hospital steward had left a vacancy to which W. H. Perry of Co. G had been promoted.

As for Co. G they kept as cool as possible. While those boys were not engaged in gathering laurels they were very watchful of those already gained.

The brush at Finnegan's Camp had whetted the appetite of Co. G for gore. They had fired four or five rounds at long range and unhorsed several johnnies. Quite an achievement in the Department of the South.

To work off their surplus ardor, or else to prevent their getting too fat and indolent, on the 1st of July, loaded down with cartridges and rations, the regiment marched aboard a steamer at dark and in the morning of the 2nd found themselves on the North Edisto river, and landed near Rockville, on John's Island. Co. G was soon on familiar ground. For the next few days the progress up John's Island was made under a scorching sun, estimated at 110 degrees in the shade (compared with previous observations). By July 5th the expedition was within six miles of Charleston. There had been but little resistance, although considerable powder had been burned.

On a foggy morning at daybreak of the 9th the rebels advanced in force. Capt. McWilliams and Lieut. Forbes, with detachments from the 157th held the center of the picket line until nearly surrounded.

Then, as customary in the Department, the forces of the expedition were "withdrawn in good order" and returned to their respective camps.

Did Gilmore or Foster ever wish to capture Charleston? Did the War Department desire its capture? Enough men composed that expedition (some five or six thousand troops) to have made a telling dash and if properly supported by the navy, a permanent footing might have been established quite near the city. Such sneaking up in the night, making faces at the surprised rebels next morning and then withdrawing "in good order," was burlesque warfare.

Unfortunately, now and then, a poor fellow fell under the rain of iron or the whistling lead, hundreds were sickening, many were dying on those desolate sands.

And while the boys were enduring such mock warfare, the dear ones at home thought of them only as their soldiers. One of the war poets sang—

"We sit at home, nor feel that they
  Who fight upon the distant plain
Are falling faster, day by day,
  A harvest of the slain."

Indeed, there was little poetry in life among the sand hills, no music in the roar of old ocean, and no comfort with the fleas. The subject becomes tedious; and yet the boys of Co. G must be followed until the close.

The loss in the 157th on the second John's Island raid, was one man, a prisoner. A poor fellow nick-named "Lightning," who was considered mentally unsound. It is to be hoped the rebels did not regard that man as representing the regiment, whatever they might have thought of him as a representative of the Department in general.

As to the object of the expedition, history says, Gen. Foster was trying to draw troops to Charleston and thus relieve Gen. Sherman, who was advancing on his famous Atlanta campaign. The success of the movement is not known, but it is supposed troops were sent from the rebel army. Five thousand additional enemies would have added but little to the force before Sherman and his determined troops.

July 24th Co. G were temporarily detached to guard fifty rebel officers who had been sent down from the Northern prisons to be placed under fire on Morris Island. The brig Dragoon lay out in the stream at Hilton Head. It was the duty of Co. G to see that those officers did not escape. Among them were Gens. Gardner, the former commandant at Port Hudson; Ed. Johnson, a prominent officer; also Jeff Thompson, Archer and G. W. Stuart and a long list of colonels and subordinate officers.

Co. G did their duty and remained with their charge until an exchange was effected, which occurred a few days later.

In the first days of September six hundred officers, ranging in rank from colonels to lieutenants were sent down to be placed under fire before Charleston, in retaliation for a similar piece of shrewdness on the part of the rebels. As soon as Gilmore began to throw shells into Charleston the righteous indignation of rebels in the field and their sympathizers North reached the explosive point. The idea of retaliative measures was a product of the brain of Jeff Davis. Burning cities is legitimate warfare. Confining helpless prisoners under fire is barbarous.

Those six hundred rebel officers were to be placed in a stockade on Morris Island, built between Fort Strong and batteries on Cummings Point.

On the sixth of September the prisoners were landed at the island and were transferred to their new guard, the 54th Mass., a colored regiment.

Sept. 5th the camp was struck at Hilton Head and by a very accommodating order the men were permitted to take with them to Morris Island such little useful articles as they desired, and so it came to pass that the ferryboat conveying the camp equipage was generously laden with bundles of boards, rude benches and tables, washtubs and the like. So that a few hours' work by experienced hands made the boys as comfortable as in their former camp. About all they had parted with were the few fleas.

A few words in parting and the flea is given a rest. This sand-flea is a small affair,—not the sand-flea, or chigre, of science—but a genuine flea. Co. G became very expert catching him. When a boy was struck, down went his stocking, the flea slid into the coarse meshes, usually too late. Some of the sufferers became expert and caught the little raiders in the dark. One man has been known to awaken from his sleep with two captives, one between the thumb and fore finger of each hand. Reader, believe this, it is correct. If you cannot believe the story, forgive the man, for he was sorely tried.

The flea of Sweden undoubtedly was larger and more defiant. History states the Queen Christina kept a little wee cannon for the purpose of shooting them. The cannon is to be seen at Stockholm. Co. G found no flea too large to handle easily and effectually.

Camp on Morris Island was very clean, very hot and when the wind blew, quite unpleasant from the sand blowing into the eyes. Co. G, however, had become reconciled to all denials. They amused themselves as best they could. Drank plentifully of Levi Randall's dried-apple beer, scoured their brass jewelry and traded with the colored troops; read and re-read the old newspapers, wrote a little and slept, whenever permitted. At night large details were marched to Fort Putnam or Fort Chatfield, and there spent the night, if undisturbed, sleeping soundly, while the city gun roared three times every hour. Often a brisk firing between Sullivan's Island and other rebel forts, made the place uproarious and cartloads of iron were flying about. But they became accustomed to the shelling and paid it slight attention. Only one member of the regiment was struck by the shells and he persistently exposed himself.

Details were sent up to the Point, three miles from camp, on fatigue duty working on the fortifications. One day while a party of the regiment were thus engaged the rebels opened spitefully. By noontime the boys were hungry. Punctual came Pat Matthews with a kettle of Ziba's best pea soup, and Co. G were happy. The boys of other companies waited until the firing ceased, when their food came. This is not given to reflect upon other cooks, but to illustrate Pat's indifference to danger.

When the regiment lay in rear of the battery at Gettysburg, July 1st, the air was noisy with bursting shells, the pieces striking around viciously. And during that interesting hour the men lay very close to the earth.

"Where's Co. G? Ah, there yez are." It was Pat, who had brought them his camp kettle filled with cool water.

"Pat, what the divil are ye doing here? Don't ye hear them fellers?" Thus spoke his brother Jim.

Pat cocked his ear a moment, for he was quite deaf, then turned to the boys.

"Ah, what the divil do I care for them. Say, b'ys, don't yez want some water?"

Never did Ziba allow his boys to be neglected if he could prevent. Sometimes the marching was hard for him and then the boys carried his kettle. But if any company was better served, it is not known.

Much has been written of the "Swamp Angel," a gun planted away out in the marsh on the south side of Morris Island and a mile or more from Cummings Point. The battery consisted of one gun which burst after firing twenty or thirty shots; afterwards the place was occupied as an outpost. Beyond the "Angel" battery was another post called Paine's Dock. The dock was the historic floating battery used by the rebels in 1861, when Sumter was first attacked. Proving a veritable slaughter-pen it was dismantled and abandoned and floated away with the tide and grounded on the southern point of Morris Island. It received a new name in honor of Capt. Paine, a union officer who, while scouting, was captured there. The pathway which led over the soft marsh to those points, was for two miles covered with planking. Frequently Co. G had representatives sent there on picket, who sometimes were obliged to seek refuge under Paine's Dock to escape the shells from a James Island battery known as "Bull-of-the-Woods."

There were times, when snugly protected from the heavy fire, the boys at the Point found time dragging heavily. Then the story-tellers were called upon. Hugh O'Brien was requested to narrate the trials and triumphs of the handsome cavalier and a princess, entitled "The Beauty of the W-o-r-rld." John Miller was easily prevailed upon to produce with dramatic effects, the narrow escape of a Negro from being buried in the hay-mow at "Old Harve's" (his father's) farm. For the boys needed some relaxation in the struggle for glory—slight compensation for duty well-done, and fun counted big, sometimes. History records exposures in winter's sleet, marches under a tropical sun, sleeping on frozen ground, as well as in a climate where the dew falls like fine mist—where fog rolls up dank from malarious swamps. But when the boys rehearse their stories of the war, they will cherish most the little kindnesses and words which helped to ease their burdens and drive away the gloom.

Inspections on that barren Morris Island were very trying. A man to stand for an hour fully accoutred, with knapsack strapped on his back, the dress coat buttoned close to his chin, his straps drawing his clothing tight about him—to stand thus in a hot sun on a breezeless day, is pitiful torture. Occasionally a man fell down in the ranks. And when the men returned to their quarters they were as tired as though they had been marching. Of course it would not have been the proper thing to inspect the troops in the cool of the day—that would not have been consistent with Folly Island tactics.

And so went along the duty on Morris Island. At night when at the Point on picket, the comrades remaining in camp saw the flying bombs from Sullivan's Island, like meteors, rise from the mortars and following a regulated arc, drop apparently where their comrades were stationed. At times the display was fearfully grand and then a monitor or two would steam up toward Fort Moultrie and take a hand in the excitement. Suddenly, the rebel fire ceased, the monitors and Cummings Point ceased; and all was quiet for the night, save the regular booming of the city gun.

An interesting event occurred while the 157th lay on Morris Island. It was casting the soldiers' vote. Gov. Seymour vetoed the bill allowing the soldiers to vote and it was carried to the people in the spring elections of 1864, and thus was legalized. In the district of Canastota but two votes were cast against the privilege, thus placing the western portion of Lenox on record as not only loyal, but true to their boys in the field. The vote in the regiment was three hundred and nine. Of these, Lincoln received two hundred and sixty-eight. McClellan received forty-one.

In Co. G the vote stood, thirty for Lincoln and prosecution of the war, and seven for McClellan and a patched-up peace. Co. G was willing to fight for peace, but not to vote for peace.

The ballots were supplied by the State and each one of them was enclosed by the voter, in a special envelope marked "Soldier's Vote," upon which the soldier wrote his name. That envelope was sealed and inclosed in another envelope and directed to the person who was to cast the vote.

Credit is due Col. Brown, who sent to Hilton Head and at his own expense provided ballots for the democrats of his regiment, their ballots not having arrived at the time. Whether those provided by Col. Brown were used, is not known. This statement is recorded, because there were unpleasant reflections cast upon the colonel, who was a strong republican but was nevertheless, honorable in this instance.

Those first fifty officers confined in Charleston jail and under fire of Gilmore's guns as already intimated, were replaced by six hundred Union officers. Among this last detail from the rebel prisons were Lieuts. Coffin, Powers and Curtice of the 157th. Fortunately the Union shells usually went beyond the prison and there were no casualties from that source. The placing of six hundred rebel officers under fire in a pen guarded by a colored regiment was retaliation with insult added, according to Southern sentiment. But the 54th Mass. were Northern men and were inferior, as soldiers, to none in the army. It was humiliating to men of spirit,—to Southern men taught from childhood to consider a negro little better than a brute—when they were ordered into line by colored sergeants and compelled to obey the rules. Verily, Jeff Davis was subjecting his brave supporters to hard usage.

The pen was in sight from the rebel shore, and it was rare a shell exploded near there; no prisoner was injured by shells. In one or two instances the guards fired upon some man and unoffending ones were slightly wounded. They had nearly the same rations as were given the Union officers in Charleston. Had they been guarded by white soldiers they would have been contented. At night the calcium lamp on Fort Strong lighted the Point and enabled the guards to keep the prisoners constantly in view.

Late in October the union officers having been removed to the rear of Charleston, orders came to send the rebel officers to Fort Pulaski, Ga.

The six hundred confederates had dwindled to five hundred and forty-nine within fifty days after leaving Fort Delaware. They had been under fire forty-five days.

Oct. 21st, 1864, the 157th were marched out on the beach and opened ranks. The 54th Mass. came down the beach with their prisoners, who moved in between the lines of their new guard.

Two dismasted schooners were lying at the wharf at Lighthouse Inlet, into which were marched those rebel officers. The hulks, towed by steamers and convoyed by a large war vessel, proceeded to Fort Pulaski, near the mouth of Savannah River.

It was late when the boats reached the fort dock and the hulks were anchored in mid-stream for the night.

During the night, on board the hulk where Co. G were stationed, there was quite a sensation created by the prisoners attempting to escape. They sawed a hole through the counter, or stern of the vessel, and several of them dropped through into the water. Not far distant was the salt marsh and Tybee Island; if they could have reached land they might have gotten away, some of them, certainly. But their calculations were wrong—the strong tide was running out and they were carried rapidly toward the sea.

"Halt! Halt!!" sang out Hugh O'Brien.

"Don't shoot, Captain. For God's sake don't fire!" came out of the water.

"Keep cool, gentlemen!" called out Capt. Mc-Williams.

Not much likelihood of sweating in the river.

When the patrol boat brought them on board, their teeth rattled like castanets. The dripping fellows asked for something warm, as they went down again into the hold.

In the morning they were landed at the fort and placed in the casemates. Gratings were placed in the embrasures and at the ends of the prison; heavy guards were on duty outside and inside. They were fed on clean food, had abundance of pure drinking water, received medical attendance when sick and in all respects fared very decently. And when a number of them were exchanged they sent an appreciative note to Col. Brown, speaking of him as "a gallant officer and a Christian gentleman." They included the names of Col. Carmichael and Maj. Place "and in fact, the conduct of all your officers and men has been such as to make the name of the 157th N. Y., a pleasant reminiscence to all Confederate prisoners from Fort Pulaski."

Those prisoners had complained bitterly of the treatment given them by men who had guarded them in the North. And while they were secure in all the privileges allowed them at Fort Pulaski, they understood their limits and thus avoided unpleasant results. Not one escaped while under the care of the regiment.

Duty at the fort was not severe, but vigilance was exacted of all sentries, who walked with weapons loaded. Fatigue parties brought wood from Tybee Island, a condensing engine supplied the post with water, the sutler was at hand with his varied assortment of pins, needles, combs and brushes, navy plug, gingersnaps, canned goods, etc.

Thanksgiving day came November 24th. The boys off-duty were drawn up in bright array. The proclamation of President Lincoln was read by the Chaplain, who added a prayer. A brief battalion drill followed and then dinner.

Turkeys and other fowls were scarce at the fort. For dinner, Ziba prepared such as he had in his best style. Capt. McWilliams added small, but palatable pies to the list, with a few other luxuries. Eaten as it was, from tin plates upon a rough but clean table, that was a memorable dinner. Away up in the North-country—yet, never mind. Co. G sent out over the intervening sea and land their warm greetings, for they knew there were places vacant for them, that no others could fill. Such thoughts made Co. G brace-up and take a new hold. It is a very dry occupation, soldiering for the fun of the thing.

It is now known Co. G saw both soldiering and some fun, but without the eyes of Lenox—and such eyes—upon them their service would have paled.

Monday, Nov. 28th, loaded down with five days' rations and sixty rounds of cartridges, Companies A, B, C, G and H, under Col. Carmichael, were ordered away from Fort Pulaski. Soon after sundown the little steamer left the wharf for Hilton Head, by the way of Skull Creek.

After waiting awhile, the expedition numbering about four thousand men, a battery of artillery and a squadron of cavalry, moved up Broad River.

The movement was conducted after the usual and well-established methods popular in the Department. It was the "wait-'till-'tis-dark-and-don't-say-a-word-about-it" plan. All night long the little fleet was endeavoring to feel its way through the fog to Boyd's Point, forty miles above Hilton Head. The steamers appeared to get lost. They ran awhile, then stopped. By and by whistles were heard. The spell was broken, for rebel rockets were seen rising from their outposts.

Near noon a landing was effected and the

weary men told to get a little rest.

After dark, with the 157th in the lead, and a few cavalrymen as advance guard, the monkey-work began. First the column moved a mile or two in one direction, about-faced and returned over the same road. Then did the same caper again until, near morning, the worn-out troops were halted at the junction of the Cambahee and Grahamville roads, and were told to lie down in the oak leaves and get some rest. Meanwhile, the johnnies, who had ample warning, were preparing for a reception and to serve every thing warm, next day. Their trains were heard distinctly near Grahamville and the boys of Co. G understood there was to be an entertainment in the morning.

Soon after daybreak picket-firing began. Co. G had barely time to make coffee when they were ordered to fall-in.

Col. Carmichael threw his entire detachment of one hundred and forty-two men, on the right of the road. The boys moved leisurely along in skirmish order for nearly a mile.

Meanwhile a few pieces of artillery were firing from both parties. Near noon Honey Hill was reached. The rebel redoubt there was pierced for several guns with ample breastworks for a strong force. A rebel account which gives the Union force at five thousand infantry and fifteen hundred artillery, states the forces of Gen. Hatch advanced on Honey Hill with sixteen pieces of artillery.

If Hatch had possessed much artillery he could not have used it at Honey Hill.

The road to the foot of the bluff thus sweetly named, led through swampy ground and deep ditches were on either side. On the left of the road and extending to the foot of the bluff was a dense wood, tangled with trailing briars. On the right of the road was a thick growth of scrub timber.

The main column advanced and struck the rebels. The forces of Hatch moved off to the right and ascended the rise of ground, where they formed and charged the work.

When Col. Carmichael heard the firing on his left he halted his men and sent for instructions, with the result that the Colonel was to cross over to the south side of the road, and form on the left of the line of battle.

When Co. G crossed the Grahamville road, close at hand was a brass gun in the ditch, where it lodged from a recoil in the narrow road. One piece of artillery, only, remained to assist the infantry and that was unable to accomplish great results, although it was served gallantly.

As soon as possible the 157th boys gained their position. Off to their right and evidently awaiting, was formed a full battalion of rebels. The johnnies disappeared, fell back into the woods and both parties were soon at work.

The lines on the left were not more than eighty yards apart. The men on both sides covered themselves behind trees and bushes and fought thus, with but one intermission, until sunset; that interval occurred when the 157th fell back for ammunition.

The volleys on the right and the steady firing on the left, maintained a continuous roar, for hours; and above the musketry was heard the sharp cracking reports of the brass piece in the road and the spiteful replies of the rebel pieces.

So near the redoubt were the 157th that grape and canister flew far above their heads, cutting away branches and bark which fell harmlessly to the ground. It was the rifle balls that were doing damage.

Capt. McWilliams was standing in an open space in rear of Co. G, when a ball went through his thigh. He turned very pale.

"Bully boys," said he, "give it to them."

The captain was assisted to the road and left with the surgeons.

Lieut. Forbes took command of the company. He stationed himself on the same attractive bit of grassy ground just vacated by the captain. Lead was passing through the air very plentifully.

"Give 'em hell, boys," roared Jerome, "they've shot the captain!"

The boys were deliberately at work behind their various shields. They watched for a puff of smoke and fired. Rarely was an enemy seen, but they knew they were there. The young recruits on the left of the company were just as firm as the old chaps, only a little more noisy.

"What's the matter Amos, are you hit?" asked Lieut. Forbes of Amos Avery.

"The blinkity-blam johnnies have hit my thumb," he replied, shaking his hand rapidly.

"Then go to the rear."

"Not by a mill-site!" yelled Amos, still trying to comfort his thumb. And he remained and soon was at work again. That was Amos.

About the time Amos had resumed firing, the air about the little grass-plot was fairly blue, with very positive cursing of rebels in the woods, or on the plain, high or low. Lieut. Forbes was seen spinning around on one foot ready to whip the entire Confederacy. A rebel had drawn bead on Jerome's leg and grazed his shin, giving him a painful contusion.

Then Co. G was without an officer. Lieut. Grant had been transferred to another company. In the midst of the fight he was returned to Co. G.

The boys were ordered to fall back for cartridges. The 56th N. Y. took their places. Johnney reb discovered a change in the line and drove the 56th. Col. Carmichael took his boys in on a charge and drove the rebels back farther than before. But the charge cost Co. G their last officer. Lieut. Grant fell, shot through the body.

Once more the little band settled down to their work. The same noise of battle still roared on the right. Not a foot of ground was gained, not an inch lost. Those eyes of old Lenox should have peeped into that tangled wood. They could have seen their boys as cool as if by the firesides, but with a dreadfully earnest look about them.

As darkness came on the firing ceased. A detachment of the regiment was left in skirmish line, among them Co. G. The forces were being withdrawn. Those woods, so lately echoing with strife, were now perfectly quiet. And when the main column had passed, a sergeant went from one to another of the thin line out there in the darkness, and whispered orders to quietly fall back to the road. The 157th detachment was rear guard. The johnnies did not follow. Both sides were fully surfeited with fighting for one day.

As stated, the five companies of the 157th one hundred and forty-two men, lost in that hot little fight of Honey Hill, S. C., Nov. 30th, 1864, twenty-seven men and three officers. Two of the enlisted men were fatally hurt and Lieut. Grant seriously.

The rebels claimed a glorious victory. They acknowledged they had fourteen hundred muskets and seven pieces of artillery to begin with; and later in the day, another regiment, a battery and a company of cavalry arrived. And their main force were behind works.

Hatch's men did not exceed three thousand, who with the exception of the small force on the left, fought without cover. Hatch lost in killed and wounded that day fully eight hundred officers and men and gained nothing. No comment is necessary.

The forces fell back, carrying their wounded

and bivouaced at Boyds Point under the protection of gunboats.

Co. G could now figure up the cost of the brisk little brush fight.

>Capt. McWilliams, wounded in thigh.
>Lieut. Grant, shot through side.
>Lieut. Forbes, contusion.
>Corporal C. A. Near, head.
>Amos Avery, left hand.
>John Miller, left hand.
>J. McMaster, head.
>Michael Miller, left hand.
>Nelson Kimball, groin.
>Simon Nestler, head.
>James Johnson, right thigh.

With exceptions of Capt. McWilliams and Lieut. Grant, the wounds were slight. Those officers eventually recovered although Grant was partially disabled for life. Neither returned to the regiment and thus Co. G lost two excellent officers.

Corporal Near was knocked over by a ball passing over the top of his head, shaving the hair close to the scalp in its course. Jim McMaster caught a buckshot against his forehead, he picked out the shot and went to the rear—it gave him a headache. Many of the boys had narrow escapes from bullets which struck the trees very close to them.

Charleston papers admitted the rebel loss to have been eighteen killed and eighty wounded.

The johnnies believed they had done great execution. One reb officer reported he had counted two hundred dead and eleven or twelve hundred wounded yankees left on the field. There was no use trying to tell the story, then, unless he told a big one. They must have been scared.

On the third of December a reconnoissance was made toward Partridge Hill and the force ran into a strong force of the enemy. After burning one cotton-gin the boys returned, having lost one man, badly wounded—Irwin Sayles of Co. G, whose right arm was amputated near the shoulder later in the day.

Dec. 5th a reconnoissance in force was ordered north, on the Coosawhatchie road. Three or four miles out, the enemy were seen. Col. Carmichael was ordered to throw out his men as skirmishers, extending into the woods on both sides of the road. Passing through the tangled forest one mile, the boys came to an open field covered by the Bee Creek battery, a redoubt on a rise of ground three hundred yards distant, which appeared just then abandoned.

Gen. Potter ordered the colonel to move his line toward the redoubt. Capt. Van Hoesen was ranking officer next to the colonel.

The boys moved forward in skirmish order, until within a hundred yards of the work. Something about the appearance of the place excited the colonel's suspicion. Leading up to the redoubt the ground was bare; the rebels had burned the grass. The line was halted and the colonel rode to the rear. Two or three mounted rebels, who passed around the hill, were gone and no other enemy appeared.

Col. Carmichael returned with three cavalrymen and started along the front of his line to inspect the rear of the redoubt. He had gone one-third of the distance, when the redoubt suddenly was alive with johnnies, who poured a heavy volley into the colonel and his escort. The cavalrymen very naturally turned and spurred to the rear. One of them was fatally wounded. A ball struck the flank of the colonel's horse, which reared and threw him over its head into the high weeds. Then the skirmishers opened fire.

Col. Carmichael arose from the ground and the johnnies gave him another volley and the colonel fell back into the weeds. When they saw the colonel fall the entire left of the line started to rescue him. Capt. Van Housen halted them and detailed two men, who went forward, assisted the colonel to his feet and they left the field supporting the brave, unselfish man who had risked his life for them.

So ended the Bee Creek incident so far as general interest may extend, but not so with the faithful Carmichael. Not a shot had injured him. In falling from his horse his sabre swung around under him and he was thus injured about the spine, and never fully recovered.

The same night after returning to the Point, orders came to be ready to move at midnight. Fires were lighted, by the light of which they read their newly-arrived letters, and they smoked and chatted while waiting for the order to move.

At one o'clock, Dec. 6th, the boys embarked for another river trip. Their knapsacks had been stacked and left—an army way of announcing that lively work was anticipated. At daybreak the boat moved up Broad River to Tillifinny Creek, where the men were landed in boats on Deveaux Neck. A rebel picket made a feeble demonstration, causing the boys to duck some, but they pulled steadily to the landing.

Capt. Van Hoesen threw out his men and the advance began. For three miles the skirmishing continued, the rebels displaying considerable force and disputed the progress from behind every belt of timber.

When the road leading to the railroad was reached, the line halted and formed along the edge of some heavy timber. A regiment of johnnies came yelling up the road and filing off to their right advanced through the woods. Very soon firing began at close range.

Supports were hurried up from the landing and formed in rear of the 157th. As the rebels pressed forward the 157th boys were ordered to fall back and lie on the ground, and as the rebs came out of the woods the main body of yankees gave them a few rounds, which drove them back in confusion and ended the fighting for that day.

Gen. Hatch at once began to entrench and get into position for a stay of several weeks.

In that brush the regimental casualties were eleven wounded, some of them badly. In Co. G the losses were four.

Sergt. Harvey Lindsley, left hip (contusion.)
Corpl. A. R. Barlow, left elbow.
Hugh O'Brien, right arm, slight.
Simon Nestler, left forefinger.

Dec. 9th, Capt. Van Slyke, who was sent up from Fort Pulaski, moved the 157th boys out to support a party engaged in felling trees in order to clear the range for artillery bearing upon the railroad. Supported by other regiments the 157th moved forward, drove in the rebel pickets and advanced until they were met by a severe fire of grape and canister shot. For some time they lay behind a low knoll; to raise a head was extremely dangerous.

While in that position word was sent to Lieut. Pierce (then assigned to Co. G) to advance his line. He sent back a message characteristic of the plucky boy.

"If there is any doubt as to my own personal solicitude in the matter, I will go alone. But as to ordering these boys up there to be slaughtered, I never will do so."

There they lay, a handful of men in front of a battery screened by earthworks, the lead and iron plowing the ground around them and an officer somewhere in the rear ordering an advance. But Co. G had been on Folly Island and the boys were not surprised. If an order had come for them to crawl nearer and make grimaces at the mad rebels, the Department would have been credited for smartness.

When night came on the boys crawled back out of range, having lost fifteen wounded, one of them mortally. Poor Frank Pratt of Co. G, he raised his shoulder a little too high and a cannon shot tore it away. Wm. L. Johnson of Co. G also, was slightly wounded in the side.

So ended the fighting for Co. G, in the Broad River expedition which was designed to cut railroad communication between Charleston and Savannah and thus assist Gen. Sherman. The move was a partial success for the batteries of Hatch annoyed the rebels and somewhat interfered with railway traffic.

The detachment from Fort Pulaski had lost in injured, Col. Carmichael, Capt. McWilliams and Lieuts. Grant and Forbes; and fifty-four men wounded—five mortally—and one missing, out of the one hundred and forty-two muskets, or more than one-third of their number.

Dec. 10th the detachment was ordered to provost duty at Deveaux Neck, and remained there until February, 1865. In the meantime their knapsacks were returned to them from Boyds Point, and were found to have been plundered of nearly everything valuable. The guards left to protect the property had been selected for their general uselessness, hence the result.

February 19th Co. G were roused up at daybreak and ordered to get ready to move. The 157th squad moved toward Ashepo Ferry, and there were joined by the other companies from the fort. The men had become acquainted with each other and the regiment appeared to them as one good big family. And when they met after so long separation, the larger half so clean and bright, and the smaller half so battered and rough-looking, appearances did not count in the hellos! and how-are-yous! of the hour. It was first, cheering, then a good all-round shake, and the band struck up "Hail Columbia!"

At night, after a pretty hard march they bivouaced, after dark, in a cottonfield at Edisto Ferry. The morning of the 20th, Col. Brown drew up his men and announced the occupation of Charleston by their old general, "Little Schimmel."

During the day a foraging party was sent out, returning with a cart laden with sweet potatoes, corn, poultry, hams and bacon, and a threatened famine was averted. Toward night, however, their wagons came up and with them some supplies, but not such as are most relished in a country running wild with fatness, sweetness and flavor.

The men crossed the Edisto on the railroad bridge and camped at Elliott's plantation. Before leaving on the 21st, for some reason, orders were given to fire the buildings and the column of Gen. Hatch moved out a short distance, and rested in a grove of pines. They were awaiting the arrival of the wagon train and moved on to Martin's Farm and camped. The boys were obliged to go nearly a mile to obtain water for their coffee.

On the 22d Ten Mile Station on the railroad was reached the troops burning a rice mill and several other buildings on the way. The depot buildings were burned and considerable track destroyed.

After dinner the regimental band, led by John Davis and Delos Wheeler, treated the boys to several well-rendered tunes. And the crowd of darkies who were following the troops, men and women, old and young, dressed in their plantation garb, gathered around the band, and some of them danced a "break-down." At night the column halted at Lownde's Plantation, where the boys feasted on fresh poultry and sweet potatoes.

Next day, the 23d, foraging parties were sent out, with varying success. One under Col. Carmichael, did not return until the 24th, having had a long tramp and found little. The men were getting short of rations.

On the 25th wagons reached them from Charleston and all was well. Chickens and high living did not wear as well as army rations.

February 26th, 1865, Co. G crossed Ashley River and entered Charleston. The boys expected to parade through the town, but were disappointed. They were moved over to Cooper River and quartered in vacant stores for the night.

Co. G had seen a great deal of the country and some warfare. The regiment has begun its warlike career on Bull Run where they had lost a chaplain (by retirement), they had now followed the secession hydra to its source.

On the morning of the 27th after inspection by Gen. Williams of Gen. Grant's staff, companies D, E, G, H and K took passage on a small steamer for Georgetown, S. C. A rough sea compelled the steamer to put back inside the bar. The 28th they started and reached Bull's Bay, where a head-sea compelled them to anchor. Water became scarce and boats were sent ashore to fill canteens for the men. Next day, the first of March, they reached Georgetown, an old, old town, on Winyaw Bay.

Duty at this post was outpost and town-guard duty. It was a picnic for the boys of Co. G. They cleaned-up, shone, worked very little and grew in fatness. With the easy soldiering a plentiful spicing of fun was always on foot.

When off duty considerable liberty was given the men. Occasionally some contrabrand who had offended in a slight degree was mercilessly seized and tossed on a blanket. At night the strains of Ziba's violin were heard, and when balls were given the colored people gathered at a vacant warehouse and hoed-it-down finely, their bare feet slapping the boards like shutters loose in the wind. And occasionally one of the soldiers was seen stepping out with a colored lass and dancing the hours away. Those balls were very high-toned.

And so the time passed until April 5th, when another move was to be made. Troops came up from Charleston and on the morning of April 5th the column formed and moved something like nineteen miles, to Potato Ferry, on Black River.

This expedition numbered 3,000 infantry, 80 cavalrymen and two pieces of artillery, under command of Brig. Gen. E. E. Potter. The object of the trip to the interior was destruction of property. Nothing had been heard up North, from the Department, since the fall of Charleston and there must be some excuse for keeping soldiers down there, and so, the boys were marching-on again.

Two companies of the 157th had been left at Georgetown with Major Place. In their stead two companies of the 56th N. Y., were sent to the 157th. Co. G were out with the expedition.

The night at Potato Ferry the rebs fired upon the picket of the 157th and Lieut. Miner captured two of the johnnies. The next night found the boys near Kingstree, after nineteen miles of marching over rough, swampy roads. The feet of the men were wet nearly all day, and wet feet meant blisters. The colored troops felt the severity of the marching—Co. G kept their place in column. The colored troops foraged nobly—Co. G were not allowed to forage. Consequently, the colored troops fed on poultry that night—Co. G fed on bacon.

The 7th of April two companies of the 157th led the advance, scouting and foraging, and at the night's camp on Montgomery's Plantation three days' rations were served to the men. The day's march was a busy one, of eighteen miles. Horses and mules were confiscated and many cotton-gins and presses were burned. The boys reached their camp in a smart rain storm.

April 8th the route which had thus far led in a westerly direction now deviated southerly. The rain had laid the dust and marching was more comfortable. At night they halted at Brewerton, having taken that road on account of the destruction of the bridge over Mill Creek. A detachment of the 157th supplied a provost guard for Brewerton and thus prevented looting. A heavy detail from the regiment was sent out on picket duty. The tired boys had marched eighteen miles.

On the morning of the 9th tobacco was issued to such of the men as used it, in the form of plug, which had been confiscated. Four miles out on the road they found the bridge destroyed over Pocotaligo river and a halt was ordered until a bridge of rails was laid. Soon after noon the column approached Dingles Mills, and it became known that three guns were posted near Sumterville to oppose their advance. Those guns were on the opposite side of a broad swamp, completely covering the approach by the road.

Two regiments were drawn up on the edge of the swamp and the union artillery was order up and opened on the rebels, at long range.

The 157th was then ordered to dislodge the enemy. Col. Carmichael threw forward Co. I as skirmishers and advanced into the swamp. The distance the boys traveled in that swamp was fully three-fourths of a mile. In places the water was nearly waist-deep, and logs, bogs and broken timber, tangled vines and drooping limbs, made order impossible.

When two-thirds through the swamp the rebels opened fire, to which Co. I replied with vigor. When the johnnies fired Col. Carmichael discovered that his guide had suddenly left him and to proceed further through the dark swamp without a guide was hazardous. The colonel ordered the firing to cease and halted his men. Directly the guide appeared (a Negro) stimulated no doubt by the sight of a revolver, but he resumed his place and the regiment proceeded

Soon after, Col. Carmichael called to his men to cease firing, the rebels also ceased and a voice called, "What regiment is that?"

"The 157th New York Volunteers!" replied the colonel, his voice echoing in the dismal tangle.

The rebels re-opened and began to fall back. Co. I pressed forward and gained open ground. The colonel with the head of his battalion was close behind and he halted the skirmishers behind a rail fence to await the arrival of the others. It was a hard place to stop in for a great while, as the guns in the shallow work in the hill just beyond them were passing grape and canister lively, and it made the air whistle.

While forming his men an aide on the staff of Gen. Potter came floundering out of the swamp to learn how the advance was progressing.

"Wait ten minutes, captain," replied Col. Carmichael, "and you can return by the road."

As the fire of the enemy was very annoying, the colonel waited only long enough to collect one-half his regiment and then ordered a charge on the battery. With a yell the boys sprang over the fence and in a few minutes the place was won. The rebels fled, leaving two pieces of artillery and their dead and wounded.

The honor of hardest fighting and greatest loss was with Co. I. But Co. G claimed the honor of being first inside the battery, more on account of their location in the line and not because of superiority over the other companies as fighters. Co. G claims honors and only such as are due them.

The aide returned by the road and reported to Gen. Potter, who soon appeared and warmly complimented Col. Carmichael and his men for their gallantry. Then the colonel handed over to Gen. Potter the captured rebel guns and colors. At a later day the 56th N. Y., by reason of having two companies in the assaulting regiment, claimed the flag and all the honors, which was altogether cheeky, although the 56th boys were good soldiers.

The losses in the 157th, in what is known as the Dingles Mill fight, were five killed and seven wounded. With the exceptions of two of the wounded, one from Co. A, and the other from Co. B, the loss in the 157th fell on Co. I. The two companies of the 56th lost ten; how many were killed or wounded cannot be given.

That night Co. G camped in Sumterville. The wounded were brought in and placed in a church. Charley Gray, of Co. I, 157th, and a man of the 56th, died there.

After the fight was over Col. Carmichael observed a man trying to screen himself behind a fence and one of the boys was stirring the fellow with the butt of his rifle. The colonel tapped the johnney on the head and asked him what he was doing there.

"I am only a poor preacher," he replied.

The colonel left him, saying to the boys the fellow was not worth taking.

As it happened, the wife of a clergyman invited Col. Carmichael to make her house his headquarters. She stated that her husband was not at home and feared he had been taken prisoner.

"I would rather he be killed than be a prisoner in your hands," she said.

The Colonel went to Gen. Potter's headquarters and returned without finding the missing husband. But while eating supper the subject was renewed and then the incident which discovered the preacher behind the fence, occurred to the colonel.

"Oh, yes, madam," said he, "I know him. I found him down by the woods. I didn't consider him worth taking."

Then the fire flew from the eyes of the offended woman. The more she scolded, the more the colonel was amused. He learned later (the fight occurring on Sunday) that when the alarm was given the people were at church. And this preacher, after invoking assistance from the God of battles, went forth with other home-guards to meet the bad yankees. The idea was not a bad one if he felt that way, but what could he have found interesting behind the fence? Perhaps he had dropped the thread of his discourse and was searching for his "fifteenthly, my brethren." An entertaining sight it must have been when the godly man reached his home and learned that his valor had preceded him.

Co. G did not believe in killing parsons especially if they were armed with Samson's favorite weapon. And while the subject is still warm, it will be well to speak of prayer as a military arm.

All through the North the good people were praying—Lord, Thou knowest? All over the South equally as good people prayed—Thou knowest, oh Lord? At the front Gen. Howard prayed—Send us victory, oh Lord? On the other side of the line, "Stonewall" Jackson prayed—Strengthen our arms with Thy might and bless our cause, oh Lord. And all of the invocations closed, usually, adding parenthetically—(If it be consistent with Thy Holy Will.)

Both Generals, Howard and Jackson, were exemplary Christian gentlemen. Both prayed with equal fervor, to the same God. But the Lord seemed to be on the rebel side at Chancellorsville and Howard escaped, with barely his reputation as a Christian, untarnished. Jackson was killed and the South mourned for him and their pastors proclaimed him a martyr.

Up in the North, down in the South, heartbroken mothers and widowed wives raised their tear-swept eyes in supplication for mercy. And the clock in the corner, alone replied—time! time!—so the sorrows were left to the healer, Time. And angels looked in and pitied them all. But the war went on—for it was a holy war?

The cause of the South rested on human slavery. The cause of the North was for freedom. When the war was ended it was seen that to free every eighth slave, one white man had given his life, and the lives of thousands of broken-hearted parents, wives and neglected children were not counted—there was little glory in it for them. But Charon's boat was floated on the depths of briny tears.

Co. G have been resting at Sumterville. They have enjoyed for the first time an issue of confiscated cigars, as an army ration, also raw peanuts. When the troops entered the town they found news of their approach already in type at the village newspaper office, and the yankee printers unlocked the forms and completed the report to date, issuing a number of the sheets as souvenirs.

While at Sumterville news came of the fall of Richmond and a salute of fifteen guns was fired from the captured pieces.

During the night of April 10th the enemy attacked the picket-line vigorously, but were repulsed.

On the 11th, after firing the jail and other public buildings the troops took the road. It was a terribly hot day and dust rolled up in clouds. They reached Manchester Depot early in the afternoon, the cavalry had burned the buildings there and had torn up the rails. Orders were given to camp; as no water was found they moved on a little further and pitched their shelters. Hardly had the boys settled themselves, when orders came to move three miles further, to Singletons. Co. G were patient. Had they not been on Folly Island?

Col. Carmichael was ordered out on the 12th, to advance to Statesburg and thence to Claremont. Three miles out they found the enemy and a skirmish ensued. Capt. Gates was ordered to deploy his company as skirmishers. The rebels were stubborn and the colonel sent for cavalry. Two hours went by before supports arrived, and then with the cavalry and one piece of artillery, the advance began, the boys skirmishing all the way to Statesburg. The colonel halted his men for dinner near the residence of the father of Gen. Anderson, of Fort Sumter fame. In the afternoon the force moved to Claremont and burned the railroad depot, a passenger coach and several bridges. Returning through Statesburg a quantity of cotton was set on fire. The boys returned to Singletons reaching camp at 9 p. m., thoroughly tired, having marched over twenty miles. One man in Co. K was killed.

Gen. Potter made us move on the 13th and 14th as the men were out of rations. A force was sent to Wrights Bluff on the Santee and obtained supplies.

April 15th they were again on the road. As they approached the ground where Col. Carmichael had met the johnnies a few days previous, the 25th Ohio were found hotly engaged. The 157th were thrown out on one flank and another regiment on the other flank. The rebels soon gave way, falling back firing, for two or three miles. Gen. Potter took another road and marched toward Sumterville. Rain commenced falling and came down heavily and the men, in spite of rubber blankets were soon thoroughly soaked, but they kept along, splashing through mud and water holes until camp was reached in a nice, soft cornfield. They had marched eighteen miles.

The 16th they moved again and met no opposition until afternoon when they were again opposed. The force of rebels before them were inferior in numbers, but decidedly pepperish over the destruction of their property, and they made a stubborn resistance, and finally succeeded in checking the colored brigade. Then the troops halted in the woods for the night.

Next day, the 17th, they started for Camden. At Rafting Creek the advance found the enemy posted behind rude works. The 25th Ohio passed round to the left and waded the swamp and compelled the johnnies to retire with some loss. Camden was reached in the evening and there a flag of truce was met, the authorities formally surrendering the town. Gen. Potter marched his men through the streets with colors flying and the 157th band playing "John Brown's Body."

Next morning, the 18th, the 157th was rear-guard. It was another hot and dusty march. At eleven o'clock the johnnies were found strongly posted in a swamp near Boykins Mill. The troops were drawn upon the left of the road in order of battle. Just as soon as the boys were ready to eat, the rebels came up in the rear and opened fire, the bullets pattering against the rail fence. They were searching for Co. G, of course. Col. Carmichael soon had his men thrown out, but the rebs had left and the boys returned to finish their meal.

After dinner the colored brigade attacked the rebels, but failed to dislodge them until the colored boys managed to cross over the creek and dislodged them by flanking. The colored troops lost a lieutenant and several men there.

It was dark before the main body got over the creek, and then Col. Carmichael was ordered out to meet the 32d colored regiment advancing by another road and came up with them about three miles out. The night was dark and rain began to pour and after going a few miles the regiment camped in a half-flooded cornfield. Co. G had then become reconciled to cornfields.

The 157th led the advance on the 19th. Soon after leaving camp the enemy was found but the 25th Ohio on one flank and the 157th on the other pressed them back. Reaching a large plantation a section of rebel artillery was met. The union guns were brought up but did little execution. The line was again advanced, the enemy continuing their fire as they steadily retreated for about a mile where they again posted themselves in a swamp which bordered a stream called Big Rafting Creek. The stream was too deep for fording. The 157th fell back for ammunition. Meanwhile the 102d colored regiment were sent to flank the johnnies, and succeeded in crossing. Artillery was brought to bear also and the enemy fell back upon their artillery posted nearby, and as the skirmishers appeared, opened fiercely, but they were pushed steadily for a while and then hastily retreated toward Statesburg. Col. Carmichael halted his men beyond Statesburg and with the cavalry charged the retreating rebels and captured twenty-five of them. At night the tired men camped at Singletons, the 157th having had an extra tramp by mistaking the road in the darkness and went to Middleton, only to return. They reached camp at midnight having marched twenty miles.

April 20th the 25th Ohio and the 157th went to Middleton, where they found the object of all the marching and counter-marching. Seventeen locomotives and one hundred cars were discovered, including passenger coaches and freight cars, many of them loaded with quartermaster's and ordnance stores. The guards, engineers and all hands, had abandoned the trains. Shoes were taken for such of the men as were in need, and then the cars and locomotives were set on fire. There was a lively popping when the shells began to explode.

That night Co. G slept at Medways Plantation in rear of Singletons.

At noon the column had reached Fulton Postoffice without serious trouble from the rebels. But now they were to hear good news. A flag of truce came from the rebels stating that a truce of forty-eight hours had been entered into between Gen. Sherman and Gen. Johnston and Gen. Beauregard had transmitted the same to his department.

Cheer on cheer went up from the troops. The news seemed too good to be true. All foraging was prohibited; the guns were discharged and with a white flag at the head of the column the return march was begun, and at night the men halted near a large mill, having made eighteen miles. Co. G was through fighting and the dark cloud of war was rolling away.

Gen. Potter started at once for the Santee where steamers with supplies were in waiting. Col. Brown, who thus far had led the colored brigade, was placed in command of the entire force and Col. Carmichael led the first brigade, Capt. Van Slyke the regiment.

On the 22d the home march continued. No public or private property was molested and the men were forbidden to fire unless attacked. As they approached Wrights Bluff, twenty-one sick and partially disabled men were left to make their way to the steamers, as easily they might.

At night the boys camped in the woods having made eighteen miles,—it might have been that distance was an average day's walk in Carolina. An order was issued that night to turn over the surplus horses and mules to the quartermaster. Some thirty sore-footed and bare-footed men who had been mounted, were by that order again to limp along for liberty's sake and the honor of two counties. But Co. G could well afford to do a little of the grinning-and-bearing of it, under the circumstances. Old Lenox was very near to them, and the road seemed shorter and the stars brighter than ever. And they slept sounder.

Col. Brown led his men forward with alacrity on the 23rd toward Murrays Ferry. The forenoon's marching was over a swampy region. Rations were nearly exhausted, foraging was prohibited and the route was continued to Leunds Ferry on the Santee, where boats with rations were supposed to be lying. During the day the men heard through rebel sources that President Lincoln was dead. After a rapid march of twenty-five miles they went into camp in thick woods.

April 24th the boys reached Leunds Ferry to find the boats had returned to Charleston, taking the rations with them. There they were, in a country abounding in food and a military order prevented them from foraging during the truce. Col. Brown must issue such supplies as were in his possession, so the men were marched up to a heap of corn in the ear and each man helped himself to two ears. The record does not state whether Col. Brown took two ears, perhaps he did. Certainly almost any other man in the colonel's position would have found means and fed his faithful soldiers on other than horse feed, in such a land of plenty. Col. Brown was an excellent man, only, he failed in acute discernment, sometimes.

The two ears of corn were to serve for supper and breakfast next morning. So when they started out on the 25th for Georgetown, twenty-three miles distant, the boys had swallowed their handful of corn and drew up their belts a notch or two, called it a square meal and trotted along. At one stage of the journey they marched a mile in fourteen minutes, and if they had drawn one, instead of two ears of corn, they might have done better. The real spring in their heels was the prospect of the home-march.

At noon wagons from Georgetown met them and the straps were loosened again. They were all glad to hear of the safety of the place, particularly those who, like Col. Carmichael, had left a wife there, twenty days before. Toward night, as the column drew near the town Mrs. Carmichael, escorted by Major Place and others, rode out on horseback to meet them. At 6 p. m., the boys were back in their old quarters. No more hard marching for Co. G.

Enough comment has been made upon the merits of raids, burnings and destruction generally. But this raid in particular was practically uncalled for. On the very day the locomotives and cars were destroyed, Beauregard issued his order announcing the truce. The surrender of Johnston practically ended the war. And thus thousands and tens of thousands worth of property were destroyed needlessly. But it was war, and so far justifiable. The estimate placed on property destroyed by that raid, including cotton, cotton-gins, presses and buildings, was at least one million dollars.

They brought back nearly one hundred prisoners, three field pieces and a quantity of arms and accoutrements. Also many horses and cattle. Near three thousand colored people of all ages followed the little army to Georgetown. They were poor people who had been slaves and all their worldly goods were few. Some carried everything they owned balanced in bundles on their heads. Others had horses or mules laden, and some had carts in which the chickens and the little freedmen shared the privilege of transportation. At Georgetown the crowd were served with rations for a few days and then were advised to return to the interior, as the war was over and they would thereafter be paid for their labor.

Co. G returned to duty, as of old and the time passed pleasantly. Hard marching made them feel a bit old and some of them believed that an inch or two was taken from the stature of each man, but the suspicion was not confirmed. A few had lost flesh and the tobacco chewers, who had reveled in the weed, might have gained a few pounds. Some had grown handsomer from roasting in the sun; certainly none had grown homelier. Co. G had no homely men. The only man who could have been called really homely, had deserted. Probably he was lonely.

In June Capt. Gates was sent to Florence, and Capt. Van Hoesen to Kingstree with their companies to assist in the early reconstruction plans and preserve order between the whites and the freedmen. This is noted because Capt. Gates is a Co. G boy. He is not to be forgotten for his good work in supplying the regiment with an excellent set of band instruments. It would have been a long time before those horns would have been bought by the same, or by any other means. Let Capt. Gates have full credit for all he did as he has passed away. He was a faithful soldier, a genial friend.

Col. Brown went North on leave, in June, and Col. Carmichael was left in charge.

June 19th Major Place was sent to Mount Pleasant near Charleston with five companies of the regiment. And on the 24th the remainder of the regiment joined the others at that camp.

Those men whose terms of service did not expire prior to Oct. 1st, 1865, were by general order transferred to the 54th N. Y. Veteran Volunteers.

Mt. Pleasant was, before the war, a resort for Charleston people and was then finely kept. When Co. G arrived there the place had a terribly neglected appearance. There were many pests to annoy the boys, of the day and of the night variety, so there was little comfort anywhere. There were drunken negroes strolling about and drunken whites likewise, and quarreling and fighting. It was a bad place for Co. G and the boys longed to get away from the stenches and the fleas and bad society generally, of the degenerated spot.

The muster-out rolls were completed and on the 10th of July the 157th N. Y. Vols. were mustered out of the United States service. On the same day they sailed for Hilton Head.

Co. G left Hilton Head, soldiers; they returned civilians. The freedom of the town was offered the boys while waiting for transportation. Some one in the regiment got into trouble, for which the whole of them were to do penance.

They were marched aboard a steamer and a schooner and anchored two miles out in the harbor. They lay there four days rocked on the bosom of the waters.

On the 15th of July the regiment were transferred to the steamers Gen. Custer and Clyde and steamed for the North.

Co. G were with the party on the Gen. Custer, an old, worn-out hulk with new paint and a newer name. Off Cape Hateras the old trap threatened to go down. Her crew were afraid she would go to the bottom. The crew worked the pumps and the soldiers worked the pumps to keep afloat. The winds raved and the boys kept on pumping until they weathered the stormy cape. Who shall be so bold as to deny that the buoyant hopes of Co. G did not lighten the vessel considerably?

On the 19th the boys landed at a North River dock in New York, and marched to the Soldier's Rest on Howard St., and were fed.

July 20th, headed by their own band and escorted by policemen and small boys, the regiment moved through Broadway. The men made a nice appearance in clean uniforms, brasses and guns and the ladies smiled upon them, and the men waved their hats to them, and their uncles,

Aaron, Levi and others who sold clothing cheap, sadly turned away, for the boys were leaving the city.

A steamboat was waiting at the dock to carry the boys to Albany, where they arrived safely early on the morning of July 21st.

It was then fix-up and prim-up, as the good people of Canastota had obtained permission for the train carrying the boys, to stop at their place.

Mike Miller once more drew out the well-thumbed picture of his better-half, as was his usual custom mornings, kissed it and said, "Goodt morning, oldt lady!" Then he proceded to darken his mustache with shoe-blacking.

Pete Cummings assumed a fresh paper collar, which he wore peacefully, after Near had taken a commission with a colored regiment.

Jim Johnson carefully twisted the corners of his newly-born mustache.

Charley Ricker stretched himself, wondering if it would be necessary to acclimate his sprouting beard and the six or eight inches of growth in stature.

Steve Harrington had changed but little, unless to grow handsomer.

Doc White had lost much sleep worrying over John Miller, while Miller sat quietly, but anxious, for he thought the slow-moving wheels of the cars were geared wrong and they were running backward.

Amos Avery, Dan Betsinger and Nick Ecker, jolly as ever, enjoyed the situation.

Jim McMaster "disremembered" seeing all the houses on the way down, as he now, on his return, saw them from the other side.

Canastota people had but three hours in which to prepare the feast, but the time was sufficient to collect a large supply of good things. The chickens soon understood there were unusual doings in town; stores of pies, cakes and doughnuts and boilers filled with hot coffee, were in waiting.

At 2 p. m., the boys arrived. The men cheered, the women who wept when they went away, wept at their return. The welcome is beyond the power of a descriptive pen. So many hearts were glad, and, alas, many were sad. All united in the grand reception.

The feast was on. Judge Barlow briefly addressed the regiment. Col. Carmichael replied in a few well-chosen words. The colonel was proud of his men.

How the good things disappeared. Two or

near the Mummasburgh road. A year or two later by general act of the state legislature all organizations representing the State of New York at the Gettysburg battle, were entitled to a monument at the expense of the state. The 157th regiment thus has two monuments there, neither of which marks the position of the battalion in the fatal wheatfield. And although several attempts have been made to secure permission of the Gettysburg Battlefield Association to change the position of one of the monuments to the proper site, thus far such efforts have failed. The reasons given for the refusal are several, but the one most potent appears to be, that "the regiment had no business out there." But it is hoped that the time will surely come when a more gratifying reply will be given to this request appreciative of that promptness and obedience to orders which brought so great disaster with so little commendation.

In 1893 the State of New York erected a noble shaft in the National Cemetery at Gettysburg. To facilitate attendance at the unveiling the State supplied transportation to all survivors who wished to attend. To each participant was voted a bronze medal commemorative of the event. Co. G was represented by a number of the boys. On

Freedmen's Bureau, and finally were discharged in April, 1866.

Soon after disbanding at Syracuse a regimental association was formed which meets each year on the 19th of September, in commemoration of the date of muster into the service of the general government. The place of meeting is selected yearly with a design to favor both Cortland and Madison counties, alternately.

The most active in organizing this Association was Col. Carmichael, who made it a duty to be present, himself, at the reunions as a comrade among comrades. And so deeply was his interest that he attended the reunion at Canastota in 1889, while suffering from a fatal illness, and against the advice of his physician, his death occurring a few weeks later.

To Col. Carmichael is due the credit for suggesting and carrying to completion the idea of a monument at Gettysburg erected by the survivors. Although the stone is not pretentious it bears upon its granite sides a record that does honor to the Empire State. In September 1886 the regimental reunion was held at Gettysburg and the monument unveiled. The stone is of gray granite and stands on Howard Avenue, near the Mummasburgh road. A year or two later by general act of the state legislature all organizations representing the State of New York at the Gettysburg battle, were entitled to a monument at the expense of the state. The 157th regiment thus has two monuments there, neither of which marks the position of the battalion in the fatal wheatfield. And although several attempts have been made to secure permission of the Gettysburg Battlefield Association to change the position of one of the monuments to the proper site, thus far such efforts have failed. The reasons given for the refusal are several, but the one most potent appears to be, that "the regiment had no business out there." But it is hoped that the time will surely come when a more gratifying reply will be given to this request appreciative of that promptness and obedience to orders which brought so great disaster with so little commendation.

In 1893 the State of New York erected a noble shaft in the National Cemetery at Gettysburg. To facilitate attendance at the unveiling the State supplied transportation to all survivors who wished to attend. To each participant was voted a bronze medal commemorative of the event. Co. G was represented by a number of the boys. On

Freedmen's Bureau, and finally were discharged in April, 1866.

Soon after disbanding at Syracuse a regimental association was formed which meets each year on the 19th of September, in commemoration of the date of muster into the service of the general government. The place of meeting is selected yearly with a design to favor both Cortland and Madison counties, alternately.

The most active in organizing this Association was Col. Carmichael, who made it a duty to be present, himself, at the reunions as a comrade among comrades. And so deeply was his interest that he attended the reunion at Canastota in 1889, while suffering from a fatal illness, and against the advice of his physician, his death occurring a few weeks later.

To Col. Carmichael is due the credit for suggesting and carrying to completion the idea of a monument at Gettysburg erected by the survivors. Although the stone is not pretentious it bears upon its granite sides a record that does honor to the Empire State. In September 1886 the regimental reunion was held at Gettysburg and the monument unveiled. The stone is of gray granite and stands on Howard Avenue,

www.ingramcontent.com/pod-product-compliance
Lightning Source LLC
Chambersburg PA
CBHW020808230426
43666CB00007B/914